How to maintain and repair your 5, 10, & 15-speed bicycle

by

Xyzyx Information Corporation
Canoga Park, California

McGRAW-HILL BOOK COMPANY

New York   St. Louis   San Francisco   Auckland   Bogotá   Düsseldorf   Johannesburg
London   Madrid   Mexico   Montreal   New Delhi   Panama   Paris
São Paulo   Singapore   Sydney   Tokyo   Toronto

23456789 SMSM 876543210

Library of Congress Cataloging in Publication Data

Xyzyx Information Corporation.
   How to maintain and repair your 5, 10, and 15 speed bicycle.

    1.   Bicycles and tricycles—Maintenance and repair.   I.   Title.
TL430.X95   629.28'8'72   78-4884
ISBN 0-07-072230-7

About this book: This Consumer Aid is written to help bicycle owners and riders keep their bicycles in top running condition. Your only requirement is a willingness to gain some familiarity with the use of common hand tools, to spend the time needed to do your own maintenance and repair, and a little bit of patience. This book covers all the maintenance procedures which can be accomplished by the bicycle owner with readily available tools.

Fully illustrated step-by-step instructions, written in an easy to follow style, are given for each maintenance task.

To best use the book, simply locate in the illustrated table of contents the appropriate part that you wish to repair, adjust, or check. The table of contents will refer you to the chapter pertaining to the part. If there is more than one version of the part—for example, one-piece crank or cottered crank—the different versions will be illustrated to give exact identification. You will then be directed to the pages with appropriate adjustment or repair procedures.

Table of Contents

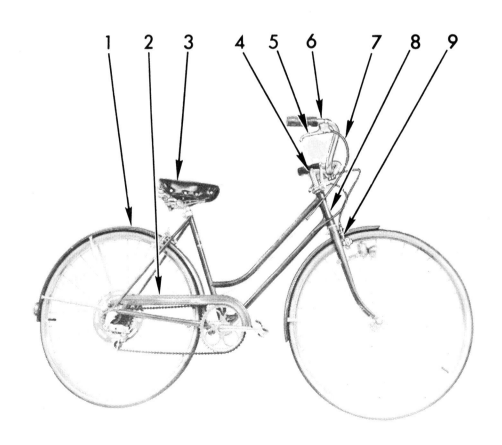

Table of Contents (Continued)

Modern bicycles, such as the derailleur models, are well engineered, precision-made machines. They are also expensive machines, ranging from about 70 dollars to well over 200 dollars. This book is dedicated to helping you get the most from your investment — both in prolonging the life of your bicycle and getting the maximum performance from the bicycle.

In order to get the most from your investment, follow the program of periodic inspection and servicing described in this consumer aid. In addition to these periodic inspections, you should inspect the bicycle any time it has been dropped to make sure that it is not damaged in a way that will be aggravated by further riding. Even a newly purchased bicycle should be thoroughly inspected to make sure that all nuts and bolts are tight and all adjustments are correct.

A word about adjustments — you will find that **care and patience are required to adjust a part precisely.** In some cases, you may have to repeat a sequence of steps several times to accomplish a correct adjustment. In less expensive bicycles, you will not achieve the precision of performance obtainable from the more expensive models. You will develop the skill and judgment to know when your particular bicycle is properly "tuned."

Having the proper equipment, supplies and tools will help ease your maintenance activity. Most bicycle shops sell tool kits, specifically for your bicycle, for less than five dollars. Because bicycle parts are manufactured worldwide but assembled under well-known trade names, a bicycle is a conglomerate of nonstandard parts. Both metric and American standard dimensions are encountered on the same bicycle. The ordinary garage "tinkerer" will usually find it worthwhile to invest in an inexpensive bicycle tool kit to supplement his original supply.

It is also a good idea to buy special bicycle lubricants from your dealer.

It is absolutely essential that you use only quality petroleum based lubricants and grease on bicycle parts. You will find that aerosol spray lubricant is a very useful aid for getting into hard to reach places, and is particularly convenient for lubricating bicycle chains. A word of caution — **do not over-lubricate.** Wipe off all excess lubricants so that you do not promote the buildup of dust and dirt deposits.

A maintenance rack will make your work easier. Several good ones are available, or you can build one yourself. We have described how to construct an inexpensive rack in the last section of this book. The maintenance rack will support the bicycle at a good working height so that you won't have to continually squat and stand while working on your bicycle.

Always keep in mind that you are handling **delicate, easily damaged parts.** Lightweight alloys have been used in place of steel for the construction of many parts, thereby shaving pounds from the weight of the bicycle. However, these alloys are generally not as rugged as steel and can be damaged quite easily. So when you are working on your bicycle always remember — **use care, don't force parts.**

In summary, to get the maximum value from your bicycle, follow these few rules:

- Obtain the proper tools and equipment — metric wrenches, if necessary, a good maintenance rack and proper petroleum based lubricants.

- Be careful when starting threads, tightening nuts, and straightening parts.

- Periodically service and inspect the bicycle.

1

PERIODIC CLEANING AND LUBRICATION CHART

Interval	Part	Maintenance Action
Weekly	Bicycle	Wipe clean with cloth.
Monthly	Bicycle	Wipe with damp cloth. Wipe dry. Polish metal surfaces. DO NOT POLISH RIMS.
	Chain	Using chain spray, lubricate chain.
	Derailleurs	Using spray lubricant, lubricate front and rear derailleur.
	Hand Brake	Lubricate cable pivot points on lever.
	Rear Wheel Hub	Using spray lubricant, lubricate freewheel.
	Seat Plastic Leather	Wipe with damp cloth. Clean with saddle soap and wipe dry.
	Selector Lever	Lubricate pivot points on lever.
Semi-Annually	Bottom Bracket	Overhaul bottom bracket.
	Front Wheel Hub	Overhaul hub.
	Headset	Overhaul headset.
	Rear Wheel Hub	Overhaul hub.

TIRE INFLATION CHART

Keep your tires properly inflated. This will reduce tire wear, protect your wheel rims, and make riding much easier and more enjoyable.

Tire Size		Air Pressure
12" X 1-3/8"		30 to 40 lbs
18" X 1-3/8"		35 to 45 lbs
24" X 2.125"		35 to 45 lbs
26" X 1-3/8"		45 to 50 lbs
26" X 2.125"		35 to 45 lbs
27" X 1-1/4"		75 to 85 lbs
27" tubular tires		
Road racing:	front tires	65 to 90 lbs
	rear tires	75 to 100 lbs
Touring:	front tires	75 to 90 lbs
	rear tires	85 to 100 lbs

FRAME AND ASSOCIATED COMPONENTS

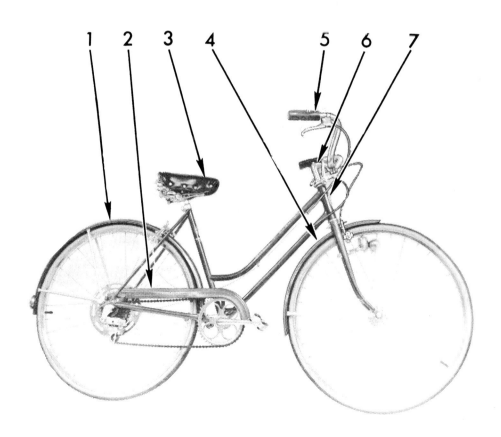

REMOVE AND INSTALL SEAT

Remove Seat.

1. Loosen nut (2). Remove seat (1) from seat post (3) by pulling up.

If not removing seat post (3), omit Step 2.

2. While holding seat post (3), loosen nut (5). Remove seat post.

REMOVE ENDS HERE

Install Seat.

If seat post (3) is not removed, go to Step 4.

Seat post (3) must be held when installing to prevent post from falling into frame (4).

3. Insert seat post (3) in frame (4). Tighten nut (5) fingertight.

4. Place seat (1) at installed position on seat post (3). Tighten nut (2) fingertight.

5. Adjust seat (Page 5).

INSTALL ENDS HERE

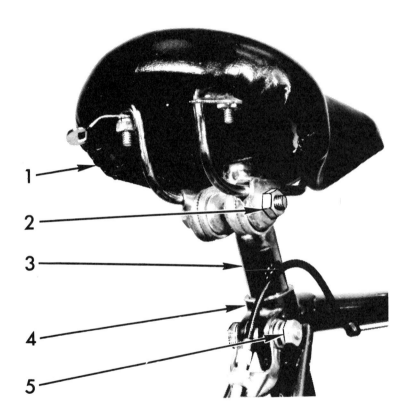

ADJUST SEAT AND HANDLEBARS

Adjust Seat.

Seat (1) should be adjusted so that at least 2-1/2 inches of seat post (3) remains in frame (4).

Seat height should be adjusted so that leg is slightly bent when pedal is in lowest position.

1. Loosen nut (7). Adjust seat height (1). Tighten nut. Loosen nuts (8).

If seat bracket (2) is not installed, go to Step 3.

2. Position seat (1) so that seat post (3) is in center of seat.

3. Adjust seat (1) so that front is slightly higher than rear of seat. Tighten nut (8).

ADJUST ENDS HERE

Adjust Handlebars.

Handlebar (9) should be adjusted so that position is comfortable and accessories may be reached easily.

Handlebar (9) should be adjusted so that at least 2-1/2 inches of stem (10) remains in frame (11).

Accessories (12) may have to be loosened.

4. Loosen bolt (6). Lightly tap bolt (6). Adjust height of handlebar (9). Tighten bolt.

5. Loosen bolt (5) or nut (13). Adjust position of handlebar (9). Tighten bolt or nut.

ADJUST ENDS HERE

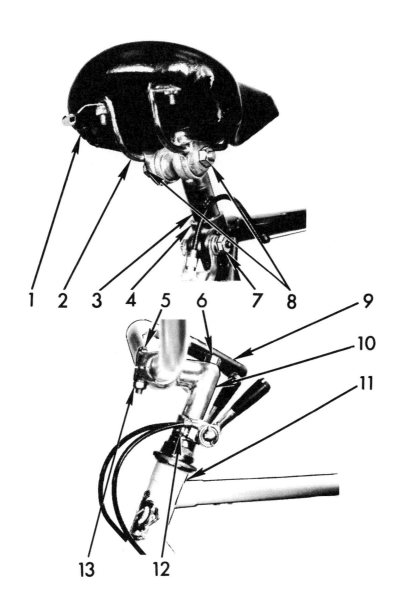

REMOVE AND INSTALL HANDLEBARS

All accessories must be removed from handlebar.

Handlebar (4) may be fastened to stem (5) with bolt (2) only or bolt (2) and nut (1).

Remove Handlebar.

1. Loosen bolt (2) or nut (1).

2. Remove handlebar (4) by pulling through clamp (3).

REMOVE ENDS HERE

Install Handlebar.

3. Place handlebar (4) at installed position in clamp (3).

Do not overtighten bolt (2) or nut (1).

4. Tighten bolt (2) or nut (1).

5. Install accessories on handlebar (4).

If handlebar is not in comfortable position, adjust handlebar (Page 5).

INSTALL ENDS HERE

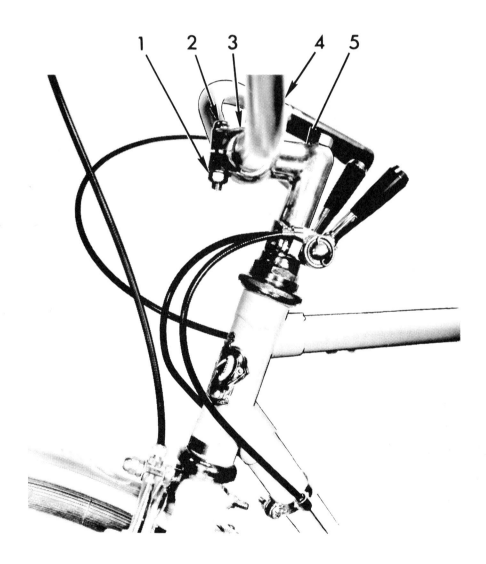

REMOVE AND INSTALL HANDLEBAR TAPE

There are two kinds of handlebar tape, adhesive and nonadhesive. If removing or installing adhesive handlebar tape, go to Page 9.

Following supplies will be needed to perform instructions in this section:

Rubbing alcohol
Adhesive tape

All accessories covering handlebar tape must be removed.

Remove Nonadhesive Handlebar Tape.

Handlebar plug (4) may be installed with or without screw (3).

1. Remove plug (4) by loosening screw (3), if installed. Pull loose end of tape (5) out of handlebar (2).

2. Unwrap tape (5) from handlebar (2).

REMOVE ENDS HERE

Install Nonadhesive Handlebar Tape.

3. Using alcohol, clean handlebar (2).

4. Check that brake lever (1) is at comfortable position.

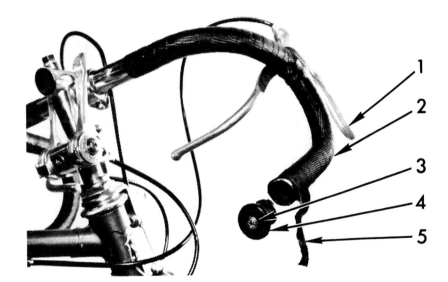

REMOVE AND INSTALL HANDLEBAR TAPE

Nonadhesive handlebar tape (1) is installed by overlapping each wrap around handlebar (2) and around base of brake lever (4). Tape should end at handlebar end (5).

1. Using adhesive tape, secure handlebar tape (1) to handlebar (2) approximately 2 inches from stem (3).

Allow 3 inches of handlebar tape (1) to insert into end of handlebar (5).

Pull tightly on tape (1) when installing.

2. Install handlebar tape (1). Insert tape into end of handlebar (5).

3. Install plug (6). Tighten screw (7), if installed.

4. Install accessories.

INSTALL ENDS HERE

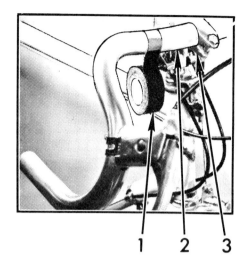

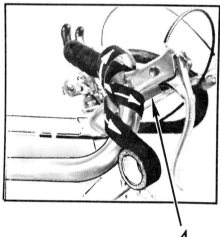

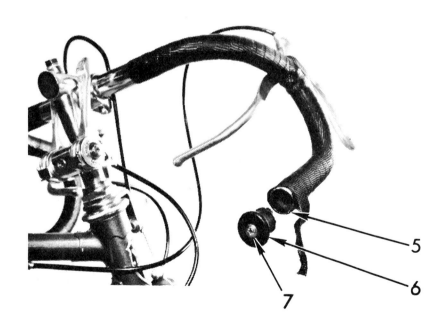

REMOVE AND INSTALL HANDLEBAR TAPE

Remove Adhesive Handlebar Tape.

Following supplies will be needed to perform instructions in this section:

Rubbing alcohol

All accessories covering handlebar tape must be removed.

1. Unwrap tape (2) from handlebar (5).

REMOVE ENDS HERE

Install Adhesive Handlebar Tape.

2. Using alcohol, clean handlebar (5).

3. Check that brake lever (1) is at comfortable position.

Adhesive handlebar tape (2) is installed by over-lapping each wrap around handlebar (5) and around base of brake lever (1). Tape should end approximately 2 inches from stem (3).

4. Beginning at end of handlebar (4), install handlebar tape (2).

5. Install accessories.

INSTALL ENDS HERE

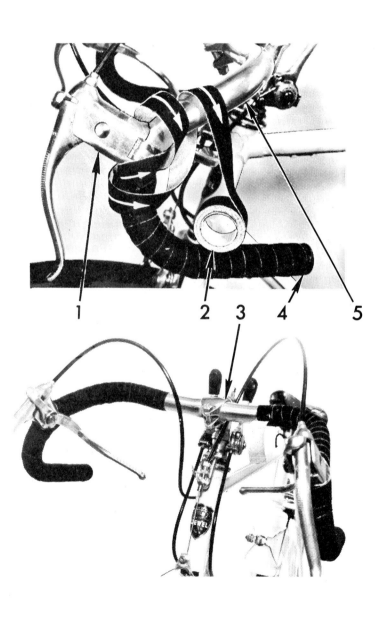

REMOVE AND INSTALL STEM

Accessories must be removed from stem (4).

Handlebar (2) must be removed from clamp (1) (Page 6).

Remove Stem.

1. Loosen bolt (3) about 1/4 inch. Loosen stem (4) by lightly tapping bolt (3) with mallet or block of wood.

2. Remove stem (4) by twisting and pulling straight up.

REMOVE ENDS HERE

Install Stem.

If stem (4) is slotted, slot (5) must line up with lug on expander cone (6).

Stem (4) must be installed at least 2-1/2 inches into frame (7).

3. Line up stem (4) with front wheel (8). Install stem. Tighten bolt (3).

4. Install handlebar (Page 6). Install accessories on stem.

INSTALL ENDS HERE

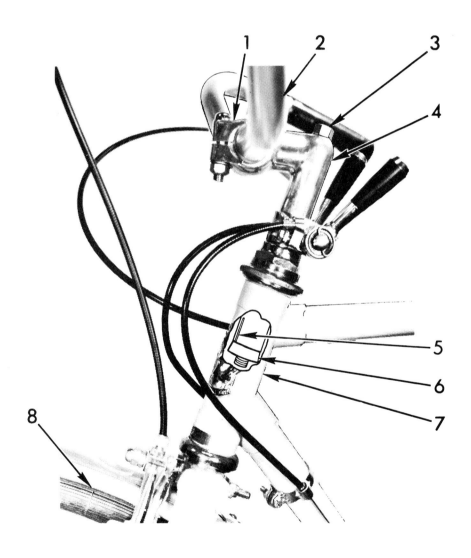

OVERHAUL HEADSET

Headsets are assembled in several different ways. Illustration shows typical assembly. Note position of all parts when removing for aid during installation.

Stem must be removed (Page 10).

Following supplies will be needed to perform instructions in this section:

Bicycle grease
Drycleaning solvent
Small bristle brush
Clean cloth

1. Remove headset locknut (2).
    Remove keyed washer (3), if installed.
    Remove cable hanger (4), if installed.

Note position of bearings (1,10) when removing for aid during installation.

Adjusting cup (5) must be carefully removed so that bearings are not lost.

Do not force top cone (6) or cup (7) when removing from headset.

2. Carefully remove adjusting cup (5).
    Remove bearings (1). Remove top cone (6).

3. Carefully remove fork (9). Remove bottom cup (7), if installed.

4. Remove bearings (10). Remove lower cone (8).

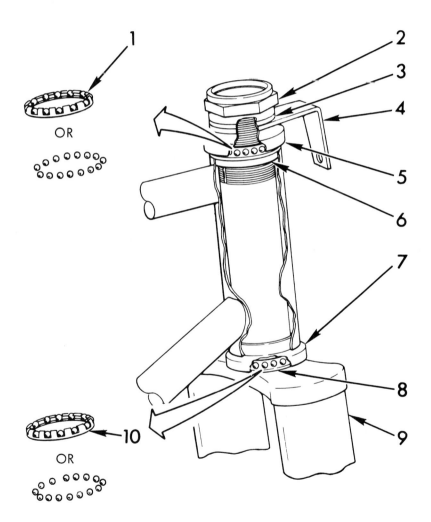

OVERHAUL HEADSET

1. Using solvent and brush, clean following parts:

   Cups (2,5)
   Bearings (1,8)
   Cones (3,6)

2. Check that bearings (1,8) are not worn or pitted.

3. Check that cups (2,5) and cones (3,6) are not worn or pitted.

   If bearings (1,8) are loose, go to Step 6.

4. Apply grease freely to all surfaces of bearings (1,8).

5. Install lower cone (6) on fork (7). Place bearings (8) on cone at noted position. Go to Step 7.

6. Apply grease freely to inside of top and bottom cups (2,5). Place bearings (1,8) in cups.

7. Place bottom cup (5) on fork (7), if removed. Carefully install fork in frame (4).

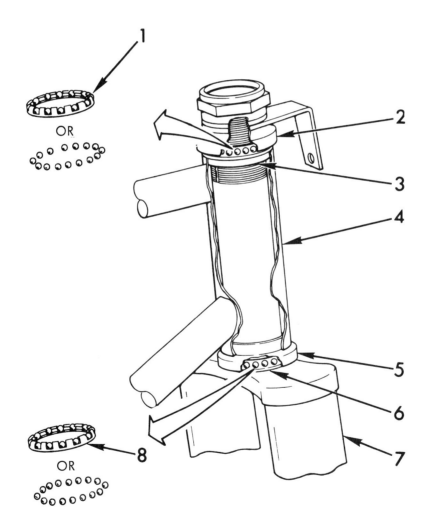

OVERHAUL HEADSET

If bearings (1) are loose, go to Step 2.

1. Install bearings (1) on top cone (6) at noted position. Go to Step 3.

2. Apply grease freely to bearing surfaces of top cone (6). Place bearings (1) in cone.

3. Install adjusting cup (5). Tighten cup until fork (7) is not loose, and does not bind when turned.

4. Install cable hanger (4), if removed. Install keyed washer (3), if removed.

CAUTION

Do not overtighten locknut (2). Bearings may be damaged.

5. Install headset locknut (2).

6. Install stem (Page 10).

OVERHAUL ENDS HERE

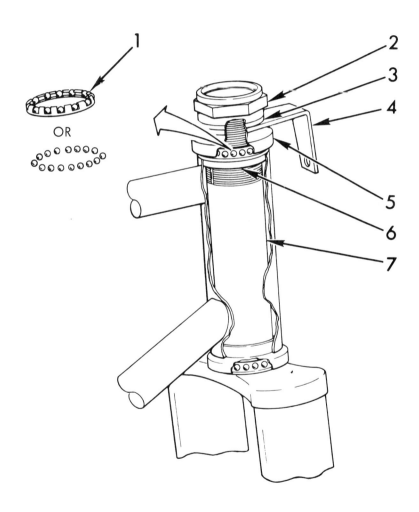

REMOVE AND INSTALL FRONT FENDER

Bicycle must be turned upside down and supported by seat and handlebars.

If attaching hardware (3) is located on inner surface of fender (2), wheel must be removed (Page 37).

Remove Front Fender.

1. Disconnect fender braces (4) by removing two screws or nuts (5) and washers.

2. Remove retaining nut (1 or 3) and washer. Remove front fender (2).

REMOVE ENDS HERE

Install Front Fender.

3. Place and hold front fender (2) at installed position. Install washer and retaining nut (3 or 1).

4. Connect fender braces (4) by installing two washers and screws or nuts (5).

5. Install front wheel, if removed (Page 38).

INSTALL ENDS HERE

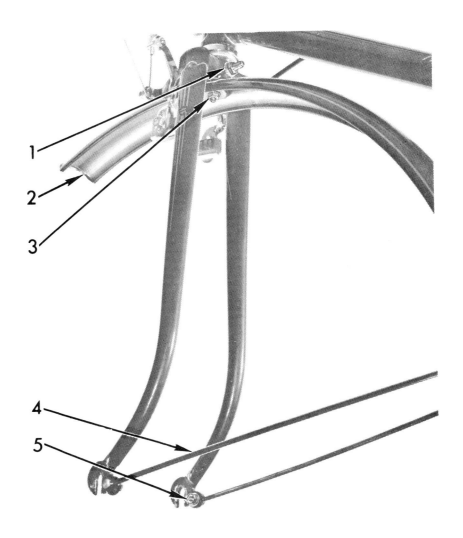

REMOVE AND INSTALL REAR FENDER

Bicycle must be turned upside down and supported by seat and handlebars.

If attaching hardware (1) is located on inner surface of fender (2), wheel must be removed (Page 43).

Remove Rear Fender.

1. Disconnect fender braces (4) by removing two screws or nuts (5) and washers.

2. Remove retaining screw or nut (1). Remove retaining screw or nut (3), if installed. Remove rear fender (2).

REMOVE ENDS HERE

Install Rear Fender.

3. Place and hold rear fender (2) at installed position. Install retaining screw or nut (1). Install retaining screw or nut (3), if removed.

4. Connect fender braces (4) by installing two washers and screws or nuts (5).

5. Install rear wheel, if removed (Page 43).

INSTALL ENDS HERE

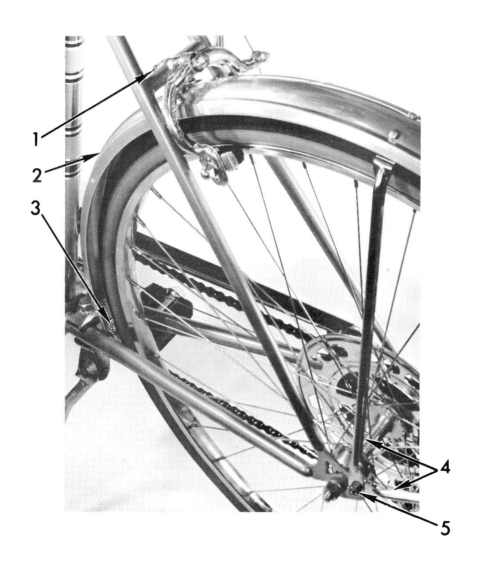

REMOVE AND INSTALL CHAIN GUARD

Chain guards (2) are fastened in several different ways. Illustration shows typical installation.

Remove Chain Guard.

1. Remove nut or screw (1) and washer at rear of chain guard (2). Remove clamp, if installed.

2. Remove nut or screw (3) and washer. Remove chain guard (2). Remove clamp, if installed.

REMOVE ENDS HERE

Install Chain Guard.

3. Install clamp, if removed. Place and hold chain guard (2) at installed position. Install washer, nut or screw (1).

4. Install clamp, if removed. Install washer, nut or screw (3).

INSTALL ENDS HERE

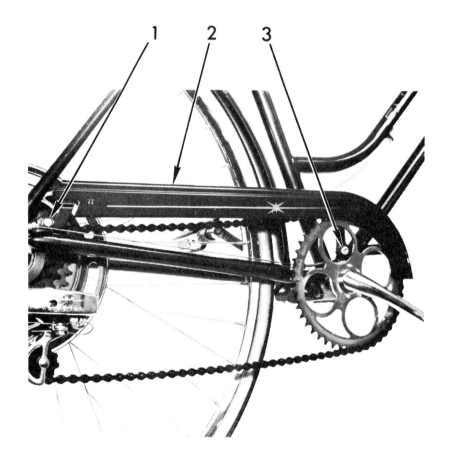

BRAKES

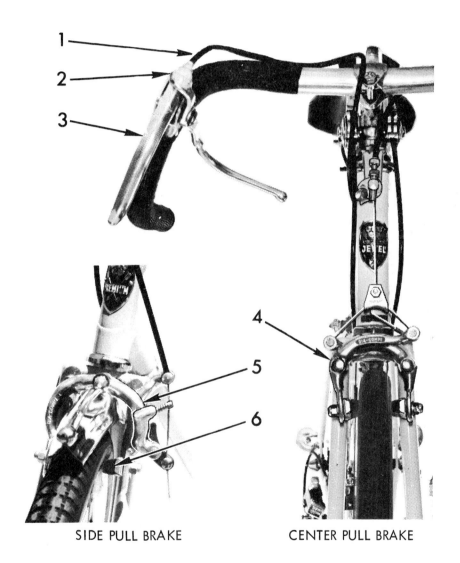

SIDE PULL BRAKE   CENTER PULL BRAKE

INSPECT, SERVICE AND ADJUST HAND BRAKES

Procedures in this section apply to front and rear center pull (5) and side pull (6) brake units.

See index on Page 17 for replacement procedures for damaged parts.

1. Check that brake lever (2) and brake unit (5) or (6) are not bent or broken.

2. Check that brake cable (4) and housing (1) are not frayed or kinked.

3. Check that quick-release (3), if installed, is securely fastened.

Raised areas on brake pads (7) must be 1/16 inch minimum.

4. Check that pads (7) are not worn or brittle.

5. Check that rim (9) is not dented, bumpy or rough.

If rim is dented, bumpy or rough, it must be repaired or replaced.

6. Rotate wheel (8). Check that rim (9) turns evenly.

If rim does not turn evenly, wheel must be trued (Page 59).

"Take your time."

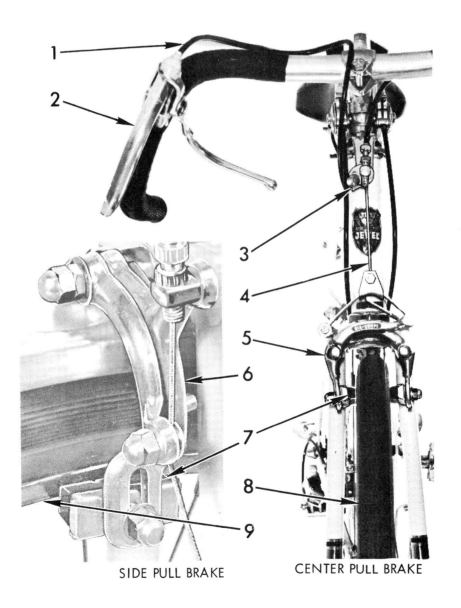

SIDE PULL BRAKE   CENTER PULL BRAKE

INSPECT, SERVICE AND ADJUST HAND BRAKES

1. Check that wheel (5) is centered between fork arms (6).

If wheel is centered, go to Step 4.

2. Loosen two axle nuts (8). Center wheel (5). Tighten nuts.

3. Check that wheel (5) is centered.

If wheel is not centered, take bicycle to dealer for repair of bent frame or forks.

4. Check that pads (3) are an equal distance from rim (2).

If pads are an equal distance, go to Step 6.

5. Loosen mounting nut (1). Move brake unit until pads (3) are an equal distance from rim (2). Tighten nut.

6. Depress brake lever (7). Check that pads (3) align evenly with rim (2) without touching tire (5).

If pads align correctly, go to Page 20, Step 1.

7. Loosen nut (4). Align pads (3) with rim (2). Tighten nut.

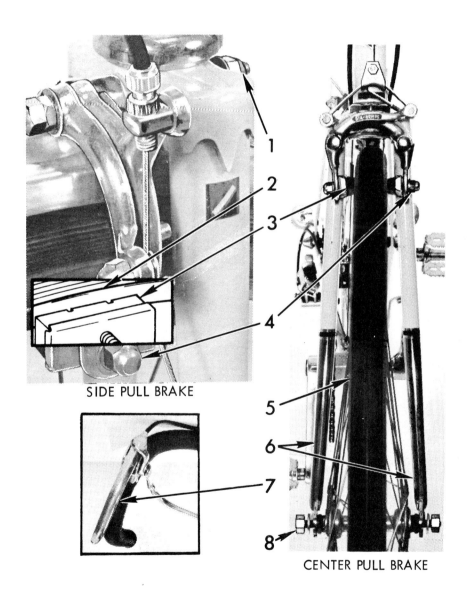

SIDE PULL BRAKE

CENTER PULL BRAKE

INSPECT, SERVICE AND ADJUST HAND BRAKES

1. Check that front edges of pads (9) are approximately 1/32 inch closer to rim (8) than rear edges.

    If front edges are approximately 1/32 inch closer to rim, go to Step 3.

2. Carefully bend brake arm (7) at pads (9) until front edges are approximately 1/32 inch closer to rim (8) than rear edges.

3. Using bicycle oil, lubricate following areas:

    Pivot bolt (4)
    Lever pivot (1)
    Brake cable end (2)

4. Depress and release lever (3) several times. Check that brake arms (7) open and close freely.

If arms open and close freely, go to Step 6.

5. Loosen locknut (6) 1/2-turn. Loosen adjusting nut (5) 1/4-turn. Tighten locknut. Repeat Step 4.

6. Check that distance between each pad (9) and rim (8) is 1/16 inch – 1/8 inch.

If distance is not 1/16 inch – 1/8 inch, go to Page 21, Step 1.

**INSPECT, SERVICE AND ADJUST
ENDS HERE**

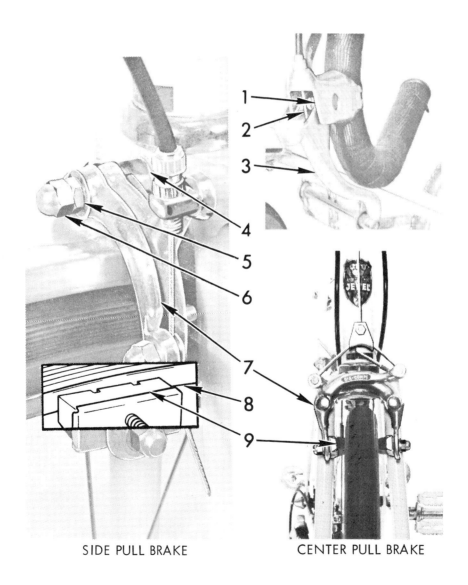

SIDE PULL BRAKE

CENTER PULL BRAKE

INSPECT, SERVICE AND ADJUST HAND BRAKES

If side pull brake (6) with adjusting screw (7) is installed, go to Page 22, Step 1.

1. Using cord, tie brake arms (4) in closed position.

2. Loosen nut (3). Pull cable end (8) until slack is removed from cable. Tighten nut.

3. Remove cord from brake arms (4). Depress and release hand brake several times.

If hand brake hits handlebar when depressed, repeat Steps 1 through 3.

4. Loosen lock ring (2) approximately four turns. Rotate cable barrel (1) until distance between pads (5) and rim (9) is 1/16 inch – 1/8 inch. Tighten lock ring.

INSPECT, SERVICE AND ADJUST ENDS HERE

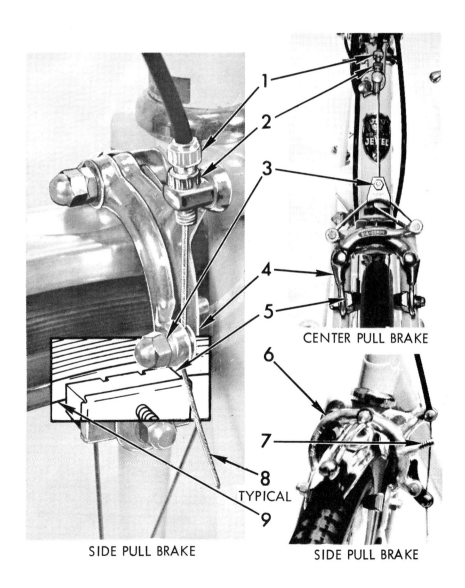

CENTER PULL BRAKE

TYPICAL

SIDE PULL BRAKE

SIDE PULL BRAKE

21

INSPECT, SERVICE AND ADJUST HAND BRAKES

1. Turn adjusting screw (2) until clearance (1) is 1/16 inch.

If pads (3) are adjusted to 1/16 inch – 1/8 inch, **INSPECT, SERVICE AND ADJUST ENDS HERE.**

2. Loosen nut on bolt (4). Pull cable end (5) tight. Tighten nut on bolt (4).

3. Depress and release hand brake several times.

4. Check that distance between each pad (3) and rim (6) is 1/16 inch – 1/8 inch. If distance is not 1/16 inch – 1/8 inch, repeat Step 1.

   INSPECT, SERVICE AND ADJUST ENDS HERE

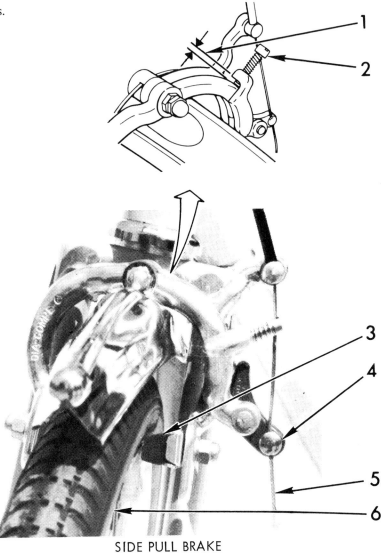

SIDE PULL BRAKE

REMOVE AND INSTALL BRAKE LEVERS

Procedures in this section apply to left and right brake levers.

Handlebar grip must be removed, if installed.

Handlebar tape must be removed, if installed (Page 7).

Remove Brake Lever.

1. Push brake quick-release lever (1) down, if installed.

2. Loosen cable end (4) by loosening nut (3). Remove cable anchor (2), if installed.

SIDE PULL BRAKE

CENTER PULL BRAKE

REMOVE AND INSTALL BRAKE LEVERS

1. Depress brake lever (1). Disconnect upper cable end (2) from lever.

2. Loosen mounting screw (3). Slide lever (1) from handlebar (4).

REMOVE ENDS HERE

Install Brake Lever.

3. Slide brake lever (1) to comfortable position on handlebar (4). Tighten mounting screw (3).

4. Depress lever (1). Connect upper cable end (2) to lever.

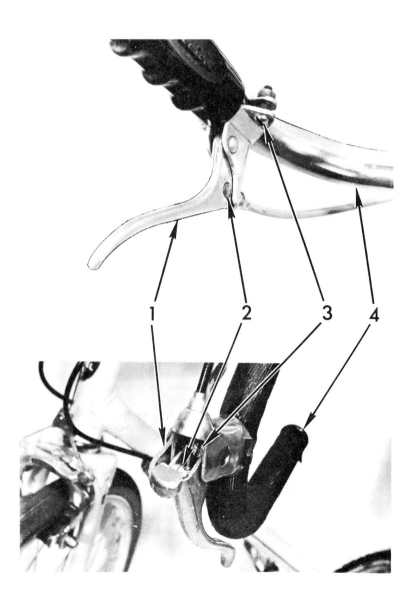

REMOVE AND INSTALL BRAKE LEVERS

If center pull brake unit (4) is installed,
go to Step 2.

1. Install cable end (10) through retaining
   bolt (8). Tighten nut (9). Go to Step 5.

2. Install cable end (7) through bolt (5).
   Tighten nut (6).

3. Connect cable anchor (2) to yoke cable (3).

4. Push brake quick-release lever (1) up,
   if installed.

5. Install handlebar grip, if removed.

6. Install handlebar tape, if removed (Page 7).

7. Inspect, service and adjust hand brakes
   (Page 18).

INSTALL ENDS HERE

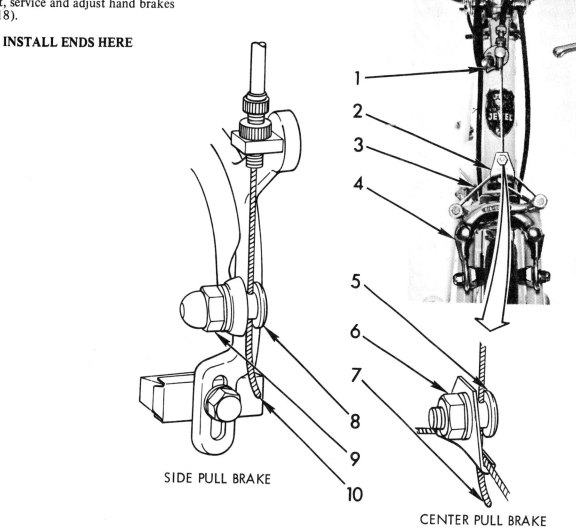

SIDE PULL BRAKE

CENTER PULL BRAKE

REMOVE AND INSTALL BRAKE CABLES

Procedures in this section apply to front and rear brake cables.

Remove Brake Cable.

1. Push brake quick-release lever (2) down, if installed.

2. Disconnect lower cable end (3) by loosening nut (6). Remove cable anchor (5), if installed.

3. Depress brake lever (7). Disconnect upper cable end (4) from lever. Remove brake cable (3) and housing (1).

If not removing cable (3) from housing (1), **REMOVE ENDS HERE.**

4. Remove cable (3) from housing (1) by pulling from upper cable end (4).

REMOVE ENDS HERE

Install Brake Cable.

If brake cable (3) has not been removed from housing (1), go to Page 27, Step 1.

5. Apply light coat of grease to cable (3).

6. Install cable (3) in housing (1).

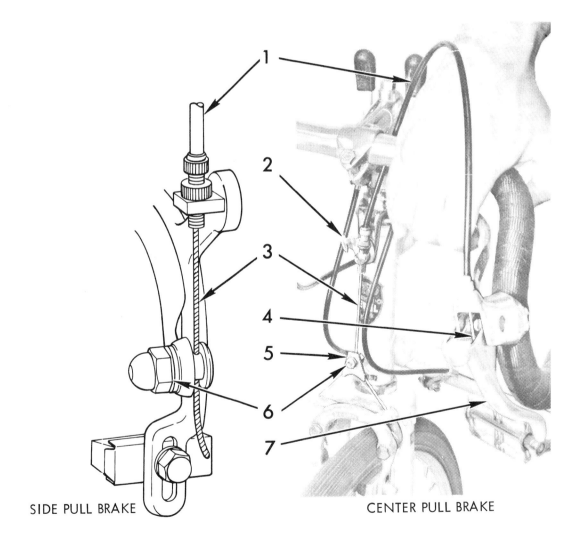

SIDE PULL BRAKE   CENTER PULL BRAKE

REMOVE AND INSTALL BRAKE CABLES

1. Depress brake lever (16). Connect upper cable end (15) to lever.

2. Install cable (6) through cable guide (3), if installed.

If installing rear brake cable, be sure housing (2) is installed in guide (1).

If center pull brake unit (13) is installed, go to Step 4.

3. Install lower cable end (12) through holder (5) and bolt (10). Tighten nut (11). Go to Step 6.

4. Install lower cable end (6) through bolt (14). Tighten nut (8).

5. Connect cable anchor (7) to yoke cable (9).

6. Push brake quick-release lever (4) up, if installed.

7. Inspect, service and adjust hand brakes (Page 18).

INSTALL ENDS HERE

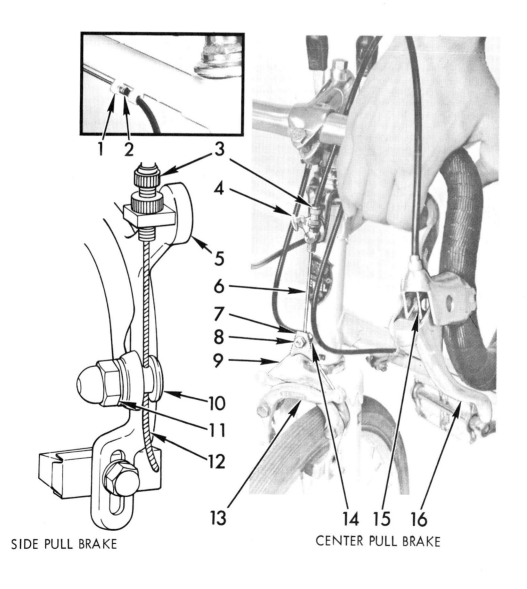

SIDE PULL BRAKE

CENTER PULL BRAKE

27

REMOVE AND INSTALL BRAKE PADS

Procedures in this section apply to front and rear brake pads.

Remove Brake Pad.

1. Remove brake pad (1) by removing nut or screw (4) and washer.

REMOVE ENDS HERE

Install Brake Pad.

Brake pad holder (3) must be installed with closed end (2) facing forward.

2. Install brake pad (1) by installing washer and nut or screw (4).

3. Inspect, service and adjust hand brakes (Page 18).

INSTALL ENDS HERE

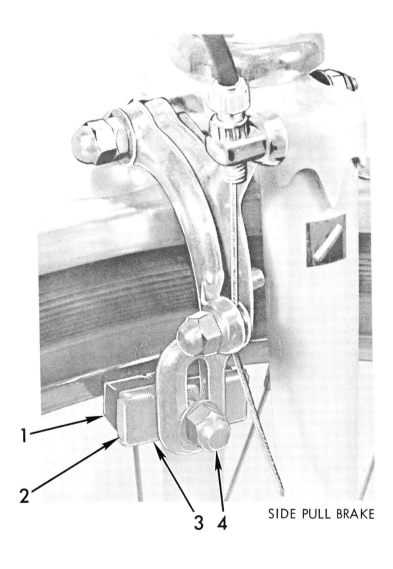

SIDE PULL BRAKE

REMOVE AND INSTALL CENTER PULL BRAKE UNITS

Procedures in this section apply to front and rear center pull brake units.

Remove Center Pull Brake Unit.

If brake quick-release (4) is not installed, go to Step 2.

1. Push brake quick-release lever (4) down. Disconnect yoke cable (1) from cable anchor (2). Go to Step 3.

Be sure cable (3) remains in bolt (9).

2. Disconnect cable (3) by loosening nut (5). Remove cable anchor (2).

3. Remove nut (8), washer, and spacer. Remove brake unit (6) with bolt (7) and spacers.

REMOVE ENDS HERE

Install Center Pull Brake Unit.

4. Install brake unit (6) with spacers and bolt (7). Install spacers, washers, and nut (8).

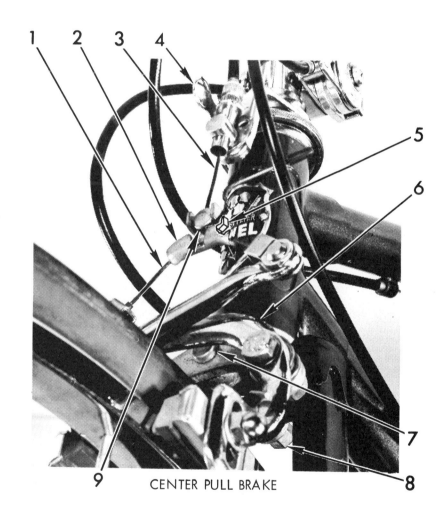

CENTER PULL BRAKE

REMOVE AND INSTALL CENTER PULL BRAKE UNITS

If brake quick-release (2) is installed, go to Step 3.

1. Install cable anchor (5) on yoke cable (1).

2. Fasten cable (3) by tightening nut (4).
    Go to Step 4.

3. Connect yoke cable (1) to cable anchor (5).
    Push brake quick-release lever (2) up.

4. Inspect, service and adjust hand brakes
    (Page 18).

    INSTALL ENDS HERE

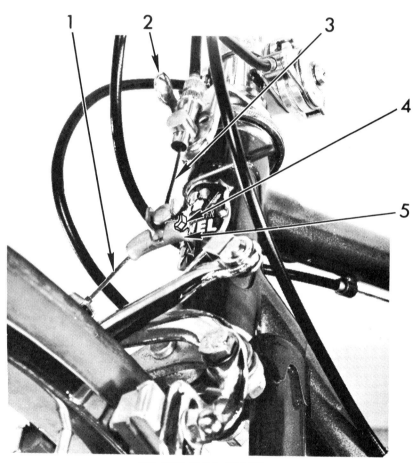

CENTER PULL BRAKE

REMOVE AND INSTALL SIDE PULL BRAKE UNITS

Procedures in this section apply to front and rear side pull brake units.

Remove Side Pull Brake Unit.

1. Disconnect cable (4) by loosening nut (6). Remove cable from holder (3).

2. Remove nut (1), washer and spacer (2), if installed. Remove brake unit (7).

REMOVE ENDS HERE

Install Side Pull Brake Unit.

3. Install brake unit (7). Install spacer (2), washer, and nut (1), if installed.

4. Install cable (4) through holder (3) and bolt (5). Tighten nut (6).

5. Inspect, service and adjust hand brakes (Page 18).

INSTALL ENDS HERE

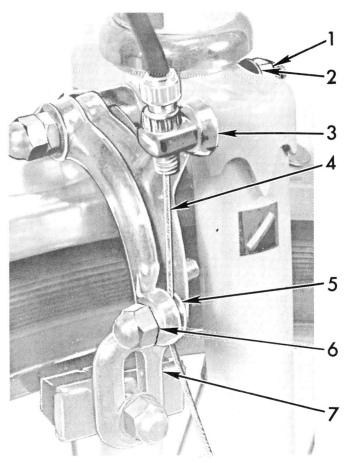

SIDE PULL BRAKE

WHEELS, HUBS, TIRES AND TUBES

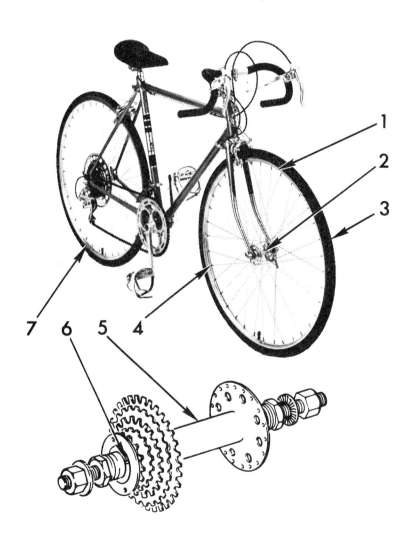

INSPECT AND SERVICE FRONT WHEEL

1. Check that wheel (1) is centered between fork arms (2).

If wheel is not centered, install wheel correctly (Page 37).

2. Spin wheel (1). Check that rim (4) turns evenly by observing that distance between rim (4) and brake pad (5) does not vary.

If rim (4) does not turn evenly, wheel must be trued (Page 59).

3. Push wheel (1) toward each fork arm (2). Check that wheel does not move.

If wheel (1) moves, front hub must be adjusted (Page 41).

4. Check that all spokes (3) are installed tightly.

If spokes (3) are not installed tightly, wheel must be trued (Page 59).

TYPICAL

INSPECT AND SERVICE FRONT WHEEL

1. While slowly spinning wheel (2), check that brake pads (1) do not touch rim (4).

If pads (1) touch rim (4), hand brakes must be inspected (Page 18).

2. While slowly spinning wheel (2), check that wheel turns freely and smoothly.

If wheel (2) does not turn freely and smoothly, front hub must be overhauled (Page 39).

3. Check that tire (3) has correct air pressure (Page 2).

4. Check that tire (3) is not worn or cracked.

INSPECT AND SERVICE
ENDS HERE

INSPECT AND SERVICE REAR WHEEL

1. Check that wheel (3) is centered between fork arms (2).

If wheel is not centered, install wheel correctly (Page 43).

2. Spin wheel (3). Check that rim (4) turns evenly by observing that distance between rim (4) and brake pad (1) does not vary.

If rim (4) does not turn evenly, wheel must be trued (Page 59).

3. Push wheel (3) toward each fork arm (2). Check that wheel does not move.

If wheel (3) moves, derailleur hub must be adjusted (Page 49).

4. While spinning wheel (3), check that brake pads (1) do not touch rim (4).

If brake pads (1) touch rim (4), hand brakes must be inspected (Page 18).

5. While slowly turning wheel (3), check that wheel turns freely and smoothly.

If wheel (3) does not turn freely and smoothly, derailleur hub must be overhauled (Page 48).

INSPECT AND SERVICE REAR WHEEL

1. Check that all spokes (1) are installed tightly.

If spokes (1) are not installed tightly, wheel must be trued (Page 59).

2. Check that tire (3) has correct air pressure (Page 2).

3. Check that tire (3) is not badly worn or cracked.

4. While riding bicycle, check that gears do not slip.

If gears slip, derailleur hub must be overhauled (Page 48).

5. While riding bicycle, check that chain (4) moves over rear sprockets (2) smoothly.

If chain (4) does not move smoothly, derailleur must be inspected (Page 63).

INSPECT AND SERVICE ENDS HERE

"Did everything check out?"

TYPICAL
1

TYPICAL
2

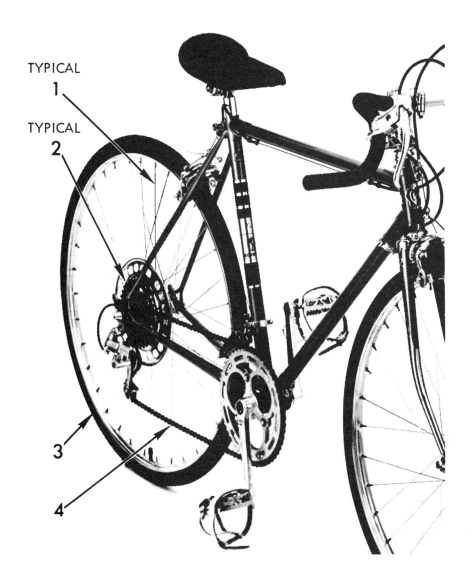

3

4

REMOVE AND INSTALL FRONT WHEEL

Bicycle must be supported by maintenance rack.

Remove Front Wheel.

1. Push brake quick-release unit lever (1) down, if installed.

If wheel has quick-release unit (3), go to Step 3.

2. Loosen two nuts (6) or wing nuts (5) at same time. Go to Step 4.

3. While holding wheel (4), loosen quick-release unit (3) by pulling lever (2) away from wheel.

4. Remove wheel (4) by pulling down and forward.

REMOVE ENDS HERE

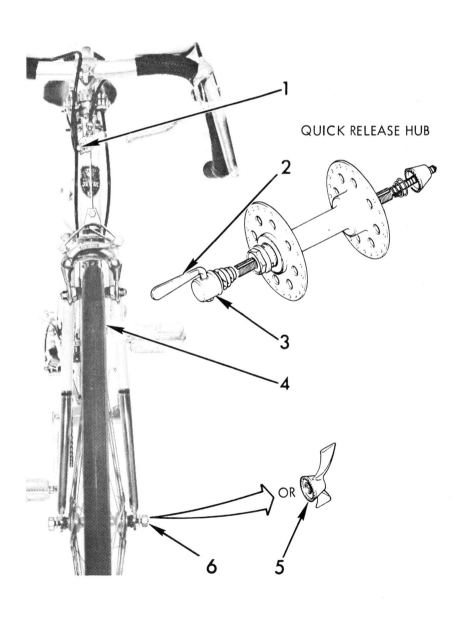

QUICK RELEASE HUB

REMOVE AND INSTALL FRONT WHEEL

Bicycle must be supported by maintenance rack.

Install Front Wheel.

If installing wheel (6) with quick-release unit, go to Step 5.

1. Place and hold axle (3) at installed position against top of fork clips (8).

2. While pressing on rim (5) with thumb, tighten opposite side nut (10) or wing nut (9).

3. Repeat Step 2 for opposite nut (9,10).

4. Check that axle (3) is against top of fork clips (8). Go to Step 7.

5. Place and hold axle (3) at installed position against top of fork clips (8). Tighten adjusting nut (2) fingertight.

6. Tighten quick-release unit by pushing lever (4) toward wheel (6).

7. Push brake quick-release lever (1) up, if installed.

8. Check that wheel (6) is centered between fork arms (7).

If wheel is not centered, go to Page 33, Step 2 to inspect wheel.

INSTALL ENDS HERE

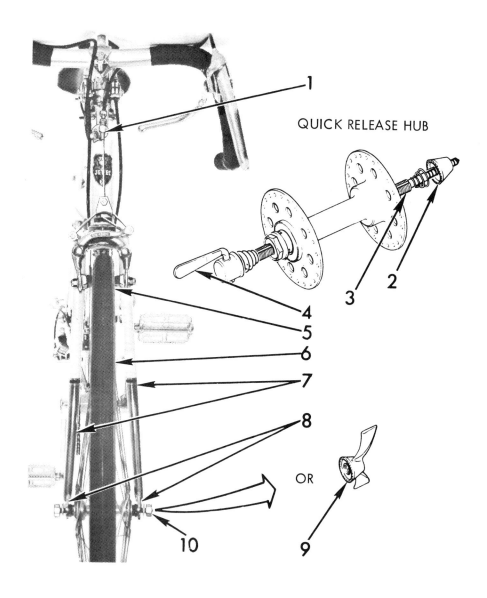

QUICK RELEASE HUB

38

OVERHAUL FRONT HUB

Following supplies will be needed to perform instructions in this section:

Bicycle grease
Drycleaning solvent
Clean cloth

Front wheel must be removed (Page 37).

Axle (9) must be firmly secured. Vise with soft jaws may be used.

If quick-release unit (15) is installed, go to Step 2.

1. Remove axle nuts (3,14) and washers. Go to Step 3.

2. Remove adjusting nut (1) and spring (2). Pull quick-release unit (15) from axle (9).

3. Place one locknut (13) in vise. Remove opposite locknut (4) and washer.

If bearings (7,10) are loose, be sure not to lose bearings when removing adjustable cone (5) and axle (9). Record number of bearings (7,10) for aid during installation.

4. Remove adjustable cone (5). Remove axle (9) from vise. Remove axle from hub (8). Remove locknut (13) and washer.

5. Measure distance from end of axle (9) to cone (12) for aid during installation. Remove cone.

6. Remove dust caps (6,11), if installed. Remove bearings (7,10).

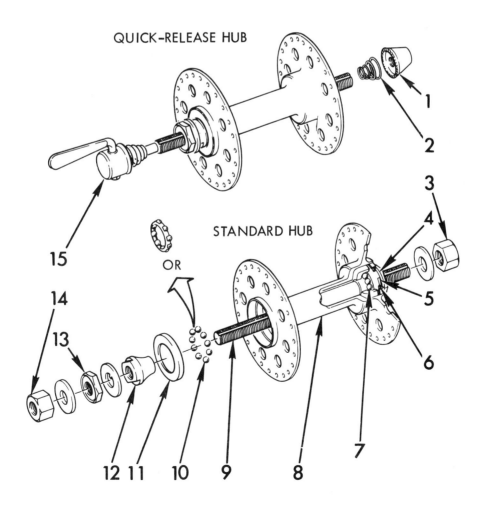

QUICK-RELEASE HUB

STANDARD HUB

OR

OVERHAUL FRONT HUB

1. Using solvent, clean all parts. Wipe all parts dry. Check that bearings (8,10) are not worn or pitted.

2. Slowly roll axle (9) on smooth surface. Check that axle is not bent.

3. Apply grease to bearing surfaces on inside of hub (3). Apply to bearings (8,10) if bearings are retained.

4. Place bearings (8) in hub (3). Install dust cap (7), if removed.

5. Install cone (4) on axle (9) to distance measured when removed.

6. Install axle (9) through bearings (8).

7. Place bearings (10) in hub (3). Install dust cap (11), if removed. Install cone (12) fingertight. Loosen cone one turn.

8. Install washers and locknuts (6,14).

If quick-release unit (15) was not removed, go to Step 9.

9. Insert quick-release shaft (17) and spring (16) into axle (9). Install spring (2) and adjusting nut (1). Go to Step 11.

10. Install washers and axle nuts (5,13).

11. Adjust front hub (Page 41).

OVERHAUL ENDS HERE

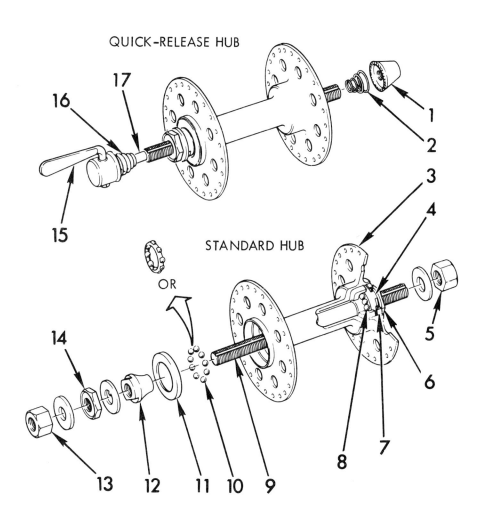

QUICK-RELEASE HUB

STANDARD HUB

OR

ADJUST FRONT HUB

Front wheel must be removed (Page 37).

Quick-release unit (6) must be removed, if installed (Page 39, Step 2).

Axle nuts (7) and washers must be removed, if installed.

Wheel must be held firmly. Vise with soft jaws may be used.

1. While holding locknut (5) firmly, move wheel (1) side to side. Check that there is no end play in axle (2).

It may not be possible, on some bicycles, to remove all end play from axle (2) and have wheel turn freely. If this is the case, some end play is allowable.

If there is no play, go to Step 3.

2. Loosen locknut (3). Tighten adjustable cone (4) about 1/8-turn. While holding cone, tighten locknut. Repeat Step 1.

3. Release locknut (5).

4. While slowly turning axle (2), check that axle does not bind.

If axle (2) does not bind, go to Page 42.

If axle binds after adjusting hub second time, front hub must be overhauled (Page 39).

5. Loosen locknut (3). Loosen cone (4) about 1/8-turn. While holding cone, tighten locknut. Repeat Step 4.

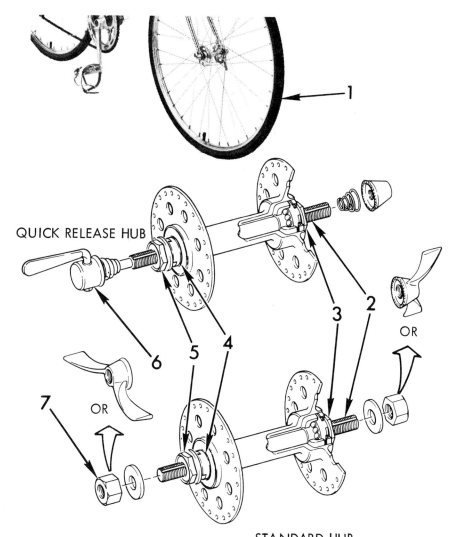

QUICK RELEASE HUB

STANDARD HUB

ADJUST FRONT HUB

1. Install quick-release unit (5), if removed (Page 40, Step 9). Install axle nuts (6) and washers, if removed.

2. Install front wheel (Page 38).

3. Place valve (1) at 9 o'clock or 3 o'clock position.

4. Release wheel (2). Check that valve (1) stops between 4 o'clock and 8 o'clock position.

If valve (1) stops between 4 o'clock and 8 o'clock position, **ADJUST ENDS HERE**.

5. Remove front wheel (Page 37).

6. Loosen locknut (4). Loosen cone (3) 1/8-turn. While holding cone, tighten locknut.

7. Install front wheel (2) (Page 38). Repeat Steps 3 and 4.

ADJUST ENDS HERE

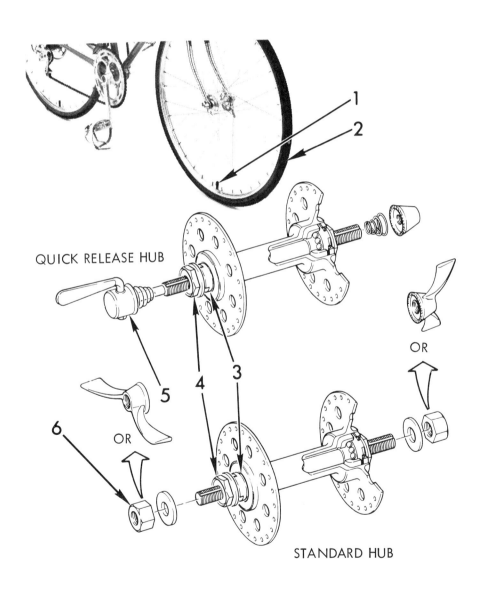

QUICK RELEASE HUB

OR

STANDARD HUB

42

REMOVE AND INSTALL REAR WHEEL

Bicycle must be supported by maintenance rack.

Remove Rear Wheel.

1. While turning pedals, push right selector lever (4) forward to place chain (5) on small sprocket (3).

   If quick-release unit (2) is not installed, go to Step 3.

2. While holding wheel (9), pull quick-release lever (1) away from wheel. Go to Step 4.

3. While holding wheel (9), loosen two axle nuts (7).

4. While pulling derailleur (8) back, push wheel (9) down and forward.

5. Lift chain (5) off sprocket (3). Remove rear wheel (9).

   REMOVE ENDS HERE

Install Rear Wheel.

If quick-release unit (2) is installed, go to Page 44, Step 1.

6. Loosen two axle nuts (7) to ends of axle (6). Go to Page 44, Step 2.

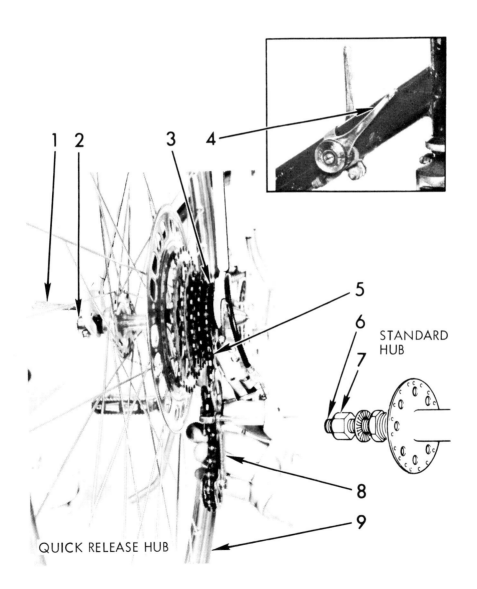

STANDARD HUB

QUICK RELEASE HUB

REMOVE AND INSTALL REAR WHEEL

1. While holding nut (7), turn quick-release unit (2) three turns counterclockwise.

2. Place chain (8) over smallest sprocket (6). Place and hold axle (3) in rear fork clips (9).

If quick-release unit (2) is not installed, go to Step 5.

3. While holding nut (7), tighten quick-release unit (2) fingertight.

4. While holding wheel (10), tighten quick-release unit (2) by pushing lever (1) toward wheel. Go to Step 7.

5. While holding right end of axle (3) against rear fork clips (9), move left end of axle until wheel (10) is centered between fork arms (5).

6. While holding wheel (10), tighten two axle nuts (4).

7. Check that wheel (10) is centered between fork arms (5).

If wheel (10) is not centered, inspect wheel (Page 35, Step 2).

INSTALL ENDS HERE

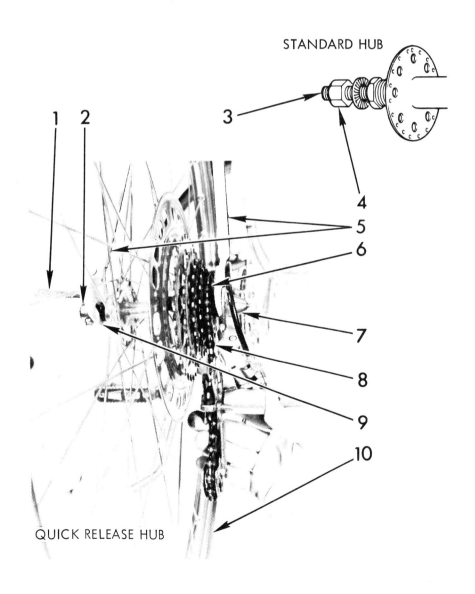

STANDARD HUB

QUICK RELEASE HUB

REMOVE AND INSTALL FREEWHEEL MECHANISM

Following tools and supplies will be needed to perform instructions in this section:

Freewheel remover (see dealer for correct type and size)
Bicycle oil
Drycleaning solvent
Clean cloth

Rear wheel must be removed (Page 43).

Remove Freewheel Mechanism.

If quick-release unit (1) is installed, go to Step 2.

1. Remove two axle nuts (2,6) and washers.

2. Remove adjusting nut (8) and spring (7). Remove quick-release unit (1) and spring (3).

3. Remove locknut (9) and spacer (10) and washer.

4. Install freewheel remover firmly in slots in freewheel (4). Install nut (8 or 6) tightly against freewheel remover.

CAUTION

Be sure freewheel remover is aligned with slots in freewheel (4).

Freewheel remover must be firmly held. Vise may be used.

5. Turn wheel counterclockwise until loose. Remove nut (8 or 6). Spin freewheel (4) off axle (5).

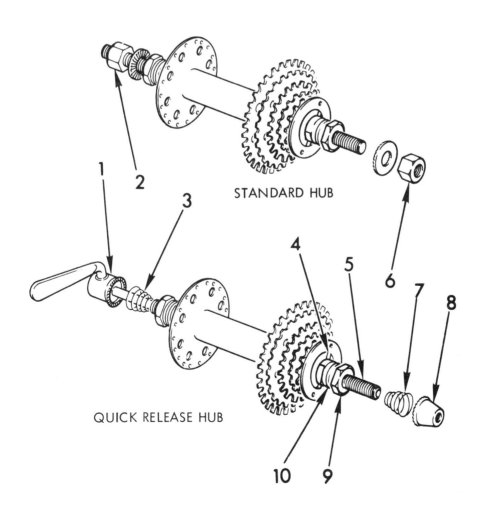

STANDARD HUB

QUICK RELEASE HUB

REMOVE AND INSTALL FREEWHEEL MECHANISM

Record order and position in which spacers (4) and sprockets (3,5) are removed for aid during installation.

1. While holding largest sprocket (3), remove chain protector (6), if installed, by turning counterclockwise. Remove sprockets (5) by turning counterclockwise. Remove spacers (4), if installed.

2. Pull remaining sprockets (3) and spacers (4) off freewheel (1).

REMOVE ENDS HERE

Install Freewheel Mechanism.

3. Using solvent, clean all parts. Wipe dry.

4. Holding inside of freewheel (1), turn outside of freewheel clockwise. Check that outside of freewheel turns freely.

5. Holding inside of freewheel (1), turn outside of freewheel counterclockwise. Check that clicking sound is heard.

6. Check that sprockets (3,5) are not bent or damaged. Check that teeth (2) are not bent, broken, or have rough spots.

If teeth (2) have rough spots, teeth must be carefully filed smooth.

7. Apply oil lightly to all parts.

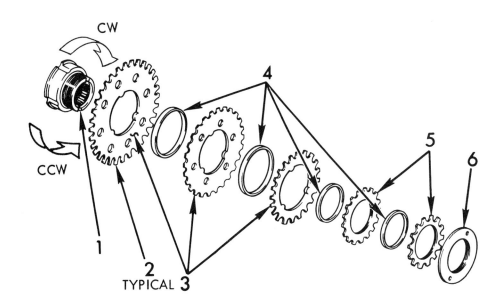

REMOVE AND INSTALL FREEWHEEL MECHANISM

1. Line up sprocket tabs (3) with freewheel grooves (1). Install sprockets (4) and spacers (5), if removed.

2. Install sprockets (6) by turning clockwise. Install spacers (5), if removed. Install chain protector (8), if removed.

CAUTION

Do not force freewheel (2) on hub (14). Threads may strip. Threads on freewheel must be oiled.

3. Carefully install freewheel (2) on hub (14) fingertight.

4. Install washer, spacer (13) and locknut (12).

If quick-release unit (16) is not to be installed, go to Step 6.

5. Place quick-release unit (16) and spring (15) in axle (7). Install spring (11) and nut (10) fingertight. Go to Step 7.

6. Install washers and axle nuts (9).

7. Adjust derailleur hub (Page 49).

INSTALL ENDS HERE

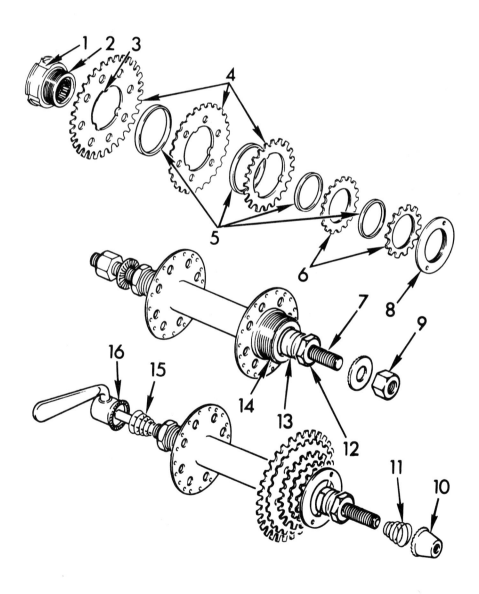

OVERHAUL DERAILLEUR HUB

Following supplies will be needed to perform instructions in this section:

Bicycle grease
Drycleaning solvent
Clean cloth

Rear wheel must be removed (Page 43).
Freewheel must be removed (Page 45).

Axle (6) must be firmly held. Vise with soft jaws may be used.

1. Place locknut (1) in vise.

2. Remove adjustable cone (10).

If bearings (5,8) are loose, be sure not to lose bearings when removing axle (6).

3. Remove axle (6) from vise.
    Remove axle from hub (7).

4. Measure distance from end of axle to cone (4) for aid during installation.
    Remove cone.

5. Remove washers (2) and locknut (1).
    Remove dust caps (3,9), if installed.
    Remove bearings (5,8).

6. Using solvent, clean all parts. Wipe all parts dry. Check that bearings (5,8) and cones (4,10) are not worn or pitted.

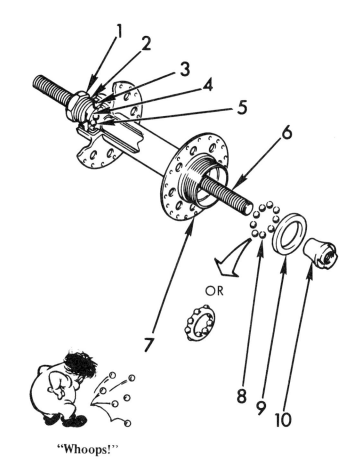

"Whoops!"

1. Slowly roll axle (6) on smooth surface.
    Check that axle is not bent.

2. Apply grease to bearing surfaces on inside of hub (7). Apply grease to bearings (5,8), if bearings are retained.

3. Place bearings (5) in hub. Install dust cap (3), if removed.

4. Install axle (6) from opposite end of hub (7). Install cone (4) on axle to distance measured when removed.

5. Place bearings (8) in hub (7). Install dust cap (9), if removed. Install cone (10) fingertight. Loosen cone 1/4-turn.

6. Install washers (2) and locknut (1) finger-tight. While holding cone (4), tighten locknut.

7. Install freewheel (Page 45).
    Adjust derailleur hub (Page 50).

OVERHAUL ENDS HERE

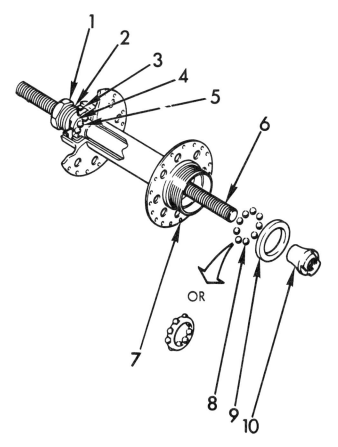

ADJUST DERAILLEUR HUB

Rear wheel must be removed (Page 43).

Quick-release unit (6) must be removed, if installed (Page 45, Step 2).

Axle nuts (7) and washers must be removed, if installed.

Rear wheel must be held firmly. Vise with soft jaws may be used.

1. Place locknut (4) in vise. While moving wheel (1) side to side, check that there is no end play in axle (5).

If there is no play, go to Step 3.

2. Loosen locknut (2). Tighten adjustable cone (3) about 1/8-turn. While holding cone, tighten locknut. Repeat Step 1.

3. Remove locknut (4) from vise.

4. While slowly turning axle (5), check that axle does not bind.

If axle (5) does not bind, go to Page 50.

If axle binds after adjusting hub second time, derailleur hub must be overhauled (Page 48).

5. Loosen locknut (2). Loosen cone (3) about 1/8-turn. While holding cone, tighten locknut. Repeat Step 4.

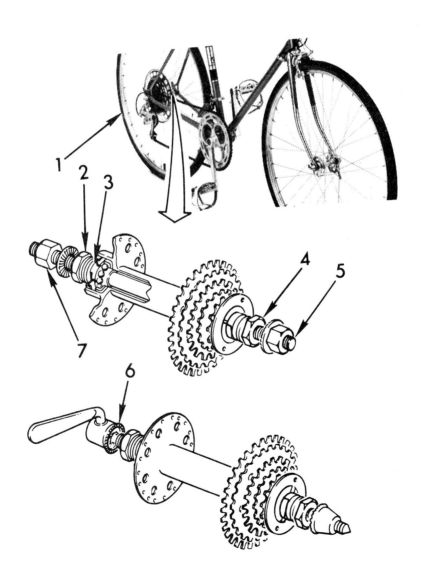

49

ADJUST DERAILLEUR HUB

If quick-release unit (4) is not to be installed,
go to Step 2.

1. Place quick-release unit (4) and spring (5) in
    axle (6). Install spring (7) and nut (8).

2. Install washers and axle nuts (3).

3. Install wheel (1) (Page 43).

4. Place valve (2) at 9 o'clock or 3 o'clock
    position.

5. Release wheel (1). Check that valve (2)
    stops between 4 o'clock and 8 o'clock
    position.

ADJUST ENDS HERE

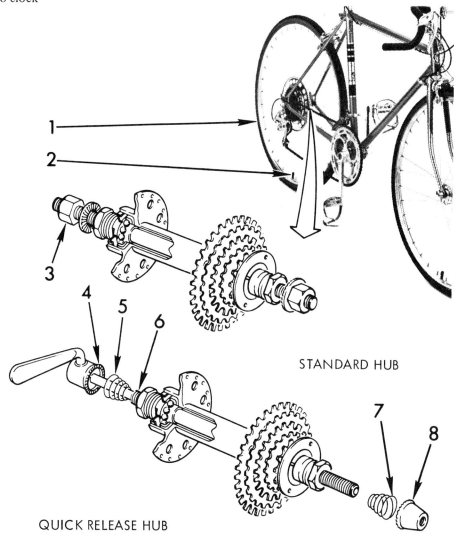

STANDARD HUB

QUICK RELEASE HUB

REMOVE AND INSTALL TIRE AND TUBE

The following tools and supplies will be needed to perform instructions in this section:

Tire gage
Tire irons
Tire pump

Wheel must be removed (Page 37 or 43).

Remove Tire and Tube.

1. Remove valve core (1). Allow tube (2) to deflate.

CAUTION

Be sure not to pinch tube when removing tire from rim.

2. Using tire irons (5), pry tire bead (3) over rim (7). Place fingers under exposed bead of tire and pull rest of bead over rim.

3. Push valve stem (6) through hole in rim (7).

4. Using tire iron (5), pry other bead (8) over same side of rim as in Step 2.

5. Pull tire (4) and tube (2) off rim together.

6. Remove tube (2) from tire (4).

REMOVE ENDS HERE

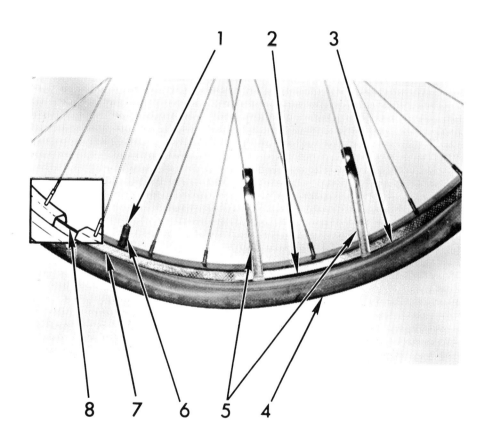

REMOVE AND INSTALL TIRE AND TUBE

Install Tire and Tube.

1. Deflate tube (6).

2. Place tire (1) on rim (2). Using tire irons (3), pry tire bead (4) over edge of rim.

3. Align valve stem (5) with hole in rim (2). Install tube (6) in tire (1). Insert valve through hole of rim.

CAUTION

Do not pinch tube when installing tire on rim.

4. Using tire irons (3), pry tire bead (4) over rim.

5. While slowly inflating tube (6), check that tire remains seated on rim (2). Refer to Inflation Chart (Page 2).

6. Install wheel (Page 38 or 43).

INSTALL ENDS HERE

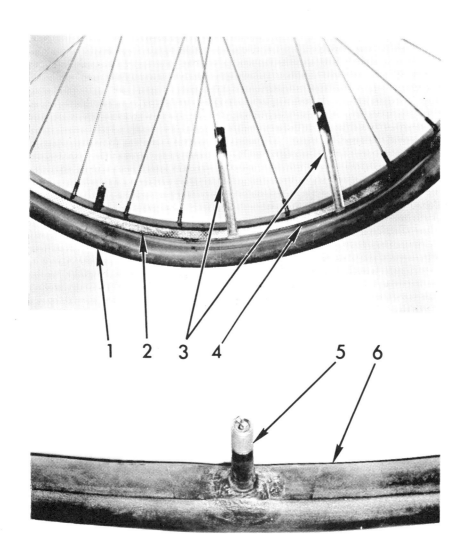

INSPECT TIRE AND TUBE

The following tools and supplies will be needed to perform instructions in this section:

Chalk
Tire pump

Tube must be removed from tire (**Page 51**).

1. Inspect outside of tire (1) for glass, metal or sharp objects.

2. Inspect inside of tire (1) for breaks, cracks or thorns.

3. Remove seal (8) from rim (5). Inspect rim (5) for protruding spokes (6) through nipples (7).

4. Inspect tube (4) for cuts or holes.

5. Install valve core (2), if removed. Inflate tube (4) to approximately 1–1/2 times normal size.

Leaking air will cause bubbles in water.

6. Place valve stem (3) under water. Check that no air leaks from valve.

If air leaks from valve, valve core (2) must be tightened or replaced.

_____

If air leaks from tube, mark location of leak with chalk.

7. While turning tube (4) in water, check that no air leaks from tube.

If tube leaks, repair tube (**Page 58, Steps 5 through 9**).

_____

If tube does not leak, install tire and tube (**Page 52**).

INSPECT ENDS HERE

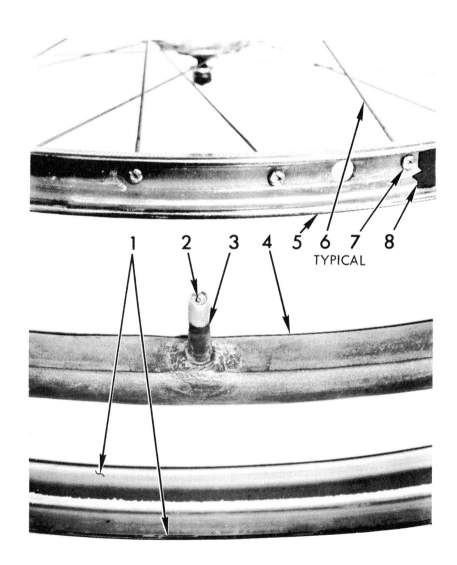

TYPICAL

REMOVE AND INSTALL TUBULAR TIRE

Following tools and supplies will be needed to perform instructions in this section:

Tire cement
Rubbing alcohol
Tire gage
Tire pump

Wheel must be removed (Page 37 or 43).

Remove Tubular Tire.

1. Remove valve cap (5). Loosen locknut (6). Release air pressure by depressing valve core (7).

2. Push tire (2) from side of rim (3) opposite valve stem (8).

3. Remove lock ring (9). Remove stem (8) by pushing out of rim (3). Remove tire.

REMOVE ENDS HERE

Install Tubular Tire.

4. Check that spokes (4) do not extend through nipples (1) on tire side of rim (3).

5. Using rubbing alcohol, clean old tire cement from rim (3). Apply thin layer of tire cement to rim. Allow to dry until tacky.

Be sure all air is out of tire (2).

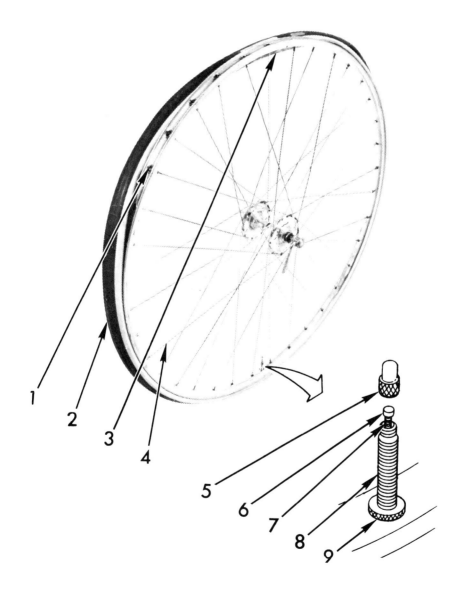

REMOVE AND INSTALL TUBULAR TIRE

1. Insert valve stem (4) in hole of rim (2).
    Place rim on soft surface.

2. With stem (4) at top of rim (2), install
    tire (1) by pushing tire over rim from both
    sides of stem.

3. Lift rim (2). Push remainder of tire (1) on
    rim with thumbs.

4. Partially inflate tire (1). Check that treads
    of tire are centered in rim (2). Check that
    tire (1) does not bulge.

5. Inflate tire to correct air pressure (Page 2).

6. Install lock ring (5). Install valve cap (3).

7. Install wheel (Page 38 or 43).

INSTALL ENDS HERE

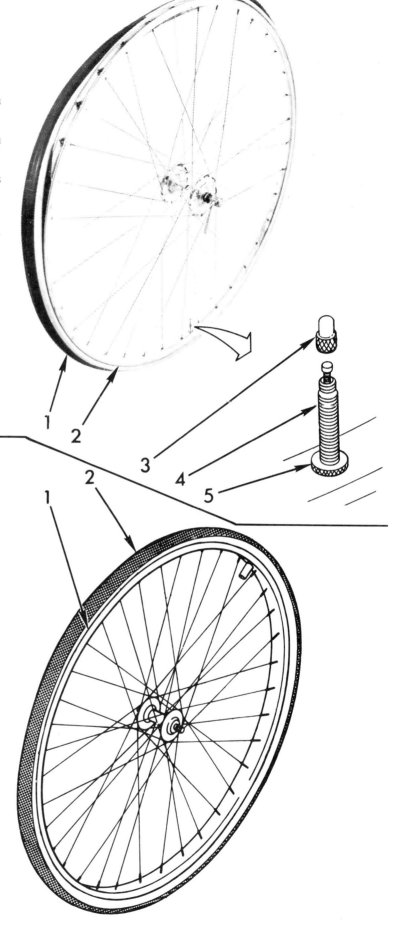

REPAIR TUBULAR TIRE

Following tools and supplies will be needed to
perform instructions in this section:

Tire pump
Tire gage
Three-point hand sewing needle
Thin tube patches
Tubular tire thread
Tire cement
Fine grit sandpaper
Talcum powder
Chalk
Tub or large container
Felt pen

Wheel must be removed (Page 37 or 43).

1. Inspect outside of tire (2) for glass, metal,
    or sharp objects.

2. Inflate tire (2) to about 65 pounds.

3. Place tire (2) in water. Slowly rotate tire
    until puncture is located. Mark puncture
    with chalk.

4. Repeat Step 3 to locate all punctures.

5. Deflate tire (2). Remove tire from rim (1)
    before continuing (Page 54).

REPAIR TUBULAR TIRE

1. Carefully lift base tape (1) from area of puncture. Using felt pen, place mark across stitching (4).

Remove stitching (4) without cutting if possible. Same holes are used for restitching.

2. Remove stitching (4). Carefully lift chafing tape (3) from around puncture.

3. While pushing aside chafing tape (3), gently pull tube (2) out about 4 inches.

4. Carefully inflate tube (2) until puncture is located. Mark puncture with chalk.

5. Thoroughly wipe tube (2) dry. Using sandpaper, lightly clean area around puncture.

6. Apply thin layer of tire cement to puncture area.

Do not continue until cement is tacky.

7. Remove backing from patch. Place patch over puncture. Press patch on tube (2) evenly.

8. Apply powder to area around patch.

9. Slightly inflate tube (2). Check that patch does not leak by observing powder. Deflate tube.

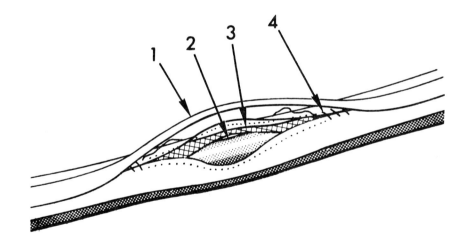

REPAIR TUBULAR TIRE

1. Check that inner tire casing (9) is not damaged.

2. Line up thread holes (3). Using felt pen, mark lines between matching holes (8).

3. Tie knot in one end of thread. Push tube (5) into place. Push chafing tape (4) into place.

4. While holding casing together, line up thread holes (3). Sew casing closed with overhand stitch (7).

5. Apply tire cement to base tape (6) and stitching in tire casing (9). Allow to dry until tacky.

6. Press base tape (6) over stitching on tire casing (9). Smooth out all wrinkles.

7. Check that all punctures are repaired before continuing.

8. Install tire (1) on rim (2) (Page 54).

9. Inflate tire (1). Refer to Tire Inflation Chart, Page 2.

10. Install wheel (Page 38 or 43).

REPAIR ENDS HERE

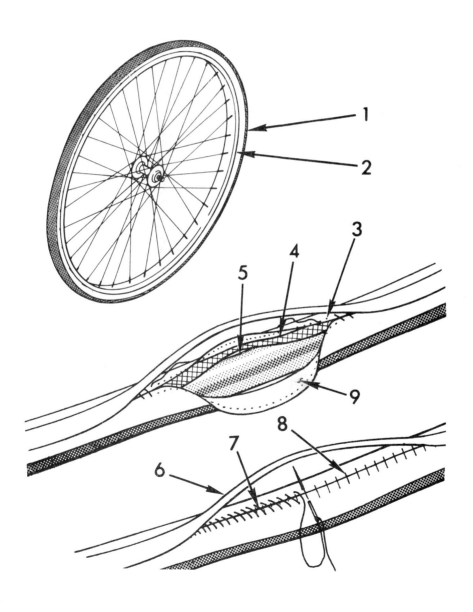

REMOVE AND INSTALL SPOKES

The following tools will be needed to perform instructions in this section:

Spoke tool

If removing rear wheel spoke on freewheel side, freewheel must be removed (Page 45).

Wheel must be removed (Page 37 or 43).

Tire and tube must be removed (Page 51).

Seal (5) must be removed, if installed.

Remove Spoke.

1. Using spoke tool (6), remove nipple (4). Remove spoke (3) through hole in hub (2).

REMOVE ENDS HERE

Install Spoke.

2. Place spoke (3) through hole in hub (2).

3. Place end of spoke (3) through hole in rim (1). Install nipple (4) fingertight.

4. Install freewheel, if removed (Page 45).

5. True wheel (Page 59).

INSTALL ENDS HERE

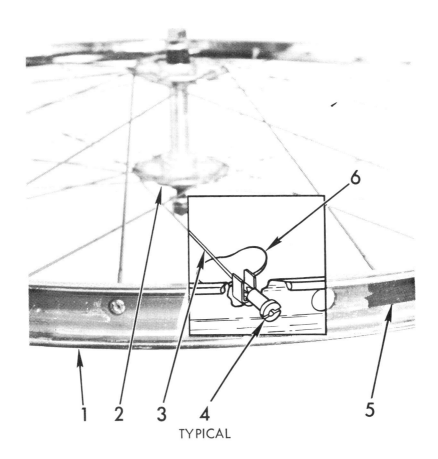

TYPICAL

WHEEL TRUING

There are many ways to true a wheel. Instructions in this section show the easiest and most economical method.

***

Following tools and supplies will be needed to perform instructions in this section:

Threaded bolt (smaller than size of slot in brake arm (4)
Two nuts
Spoke tool
File

Brake pads must be removed (Page 28).

***

Tire and tube must be removed (Page 51).
Rubber seal (9) must be removed.
Hub must be adjusted (Page 41 or 49).
Install wheel (Page 38 or 43).

***

Bicycle must be supported by maintenance rack.

1. Install nut (3) on bolt (2). Install bolt through slot in brake arm (4). Install nut (1) on bolt.

2. Start at valve hole (8). Using spoke tool, turn nipples (6) 1/2-turn only until all spokes (7) are tight.

3. Spin wheel. By adjusting nuts (1,3), tighten bolt (2) until distance from rim (5) is about 1/8 inch at closest point.

WHEEL TRUING

1. Spin wheel. Check that distance between bolt (1) and rim (2) does not vary.

If distance does not vary, go to Page 61, Step 1.

2. Spin wheel. Mark location on rim (2) that is closest to end of bolt (1).

Spokes (4) on same side of rim (2) as bolt (1) must be loosened. Spokes (5) on opposite side must be tightened.

3. Adjust four spokes (4,5) on each side of mark on rim (2) by turning nipple (3) 1/2-turn.

4. Spin wheel. Check that distance between rim (2) and bolt (1) does not vary.

If distance varies, repeat Steps 1 through 4.

"Don't rush!"

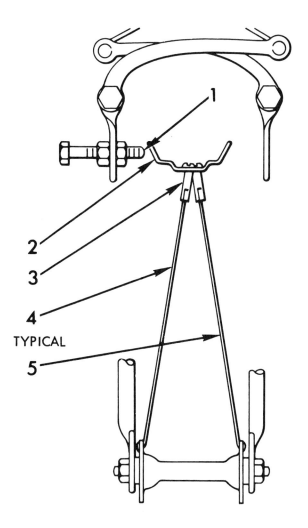

WHEEL TRUING

1. Check that spokes (4) do not extend through nipples (3).

If spokes (4) do not extend through nipples (3), go to Step 3.

2. File spokes (4) until spokes are even with nipples (3).

3. Remove bolt (1) by removing nut (2).

4. Remove wheel (6) from bicycle (Page 37 or 43).

5. Install rubber seal (5).
   Install tire and tube (Page 51).
   Install brake pads (Page 28).
   Install wheel (Page 38 or 43).

WHEEL TRUING ENDS HERE

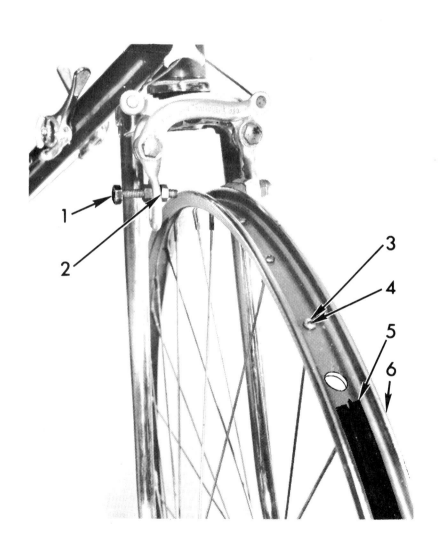

SPEED SELECTOR MECHANISMS

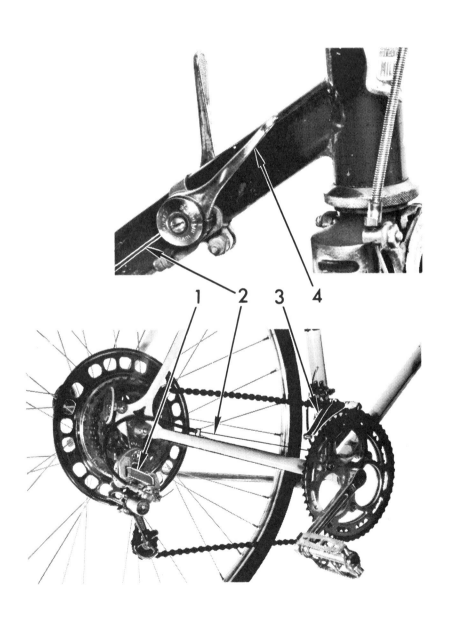

INSPECT DERAILLEURS

Procedures in this section apply to front and rear derailleurs.

Rear wheel must be supported off ground.

1. Check that derailleurs (1,3) are not bent or damaged.

If front derailleur (3) is bent or damaged, derailleur must be replaced. If rear derailleur (1) is bent, derailleur can be adjusted (Page 73). If damaged, rear derailleur must be replaced (Page 71).

2. Check that derailleurs (1,3) are clean.

If not clean, derailleurs must be cleaned and lubricated (Page 2).

3. Check that derailleurs (1,3) are mounted securely.

4. Check that speed selector cables (2) do not have excessive slack.

If cables have excessive slack, derailleurs must be adjusted (rear derailleur, Page 73, front derailleur, Page 68).

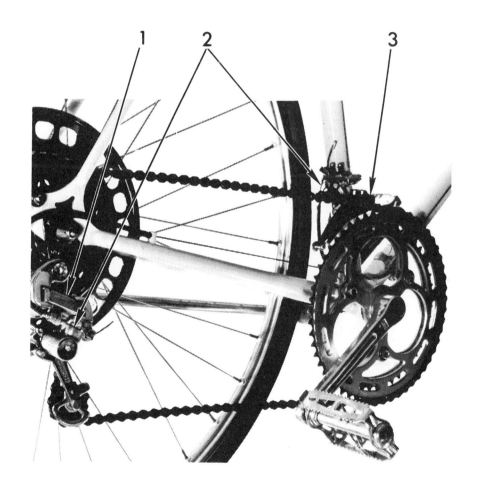

INSPECT DERAILLEURS

Movement of selector levers (1) should be stiff but not difficult.

1. Move levers (1) back and forth several times. Check levers for proper movement.

If levers move properly, go to Step 3.

Adjustment screw or nut (2) is turned clockwise to stiffen movement of lever (1). Screw or nut is turned counterclockwise to loosen movement.

2. Adjust screw or nut (2) until movement of lever (1) is stiff but not difficult.

3. While turning pedals (4), move levers (1) to each gear position. Check that chain (3) changes gears smoothly.

If chain does not change gears smoothly, front derailleur must be adjusted (Page 68).

TYPICAL

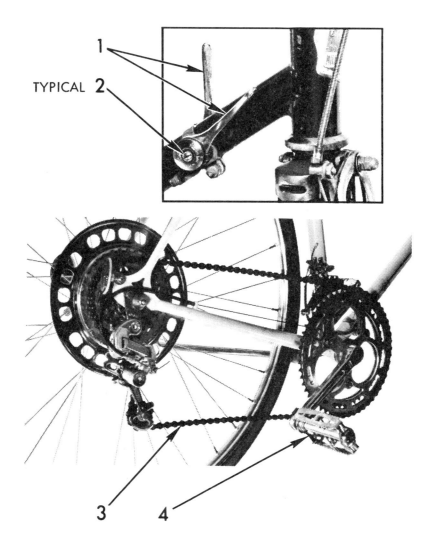

64

INSPECT DERAILLEURS

1. While turning pedals (7), move levers (1) to each gear position. Check that chain (2) does not rub chain guide (5) or chain cage (4).

If chain rubs, derailleurs must be adjusted (rear derailleur, Page 73, front derailleur, Page 68).

2. While riding bicycle, move levers (1) to each gear position. Check that chain (2) engages and stays on chainwheel (6) and sprocket (3).

If chain does not stay on both chainwheel (6) and sprocket (3), front derailleur must be adjusted (Page 68).
───────────
If chain does not stay on chainwheel (6) only, front derailleur must be adjusted (Page 68).

If chain does not stay on sprocket (3) only, rear derailleur must be adjusted (Page 73).

INSPECT ENDS HERE

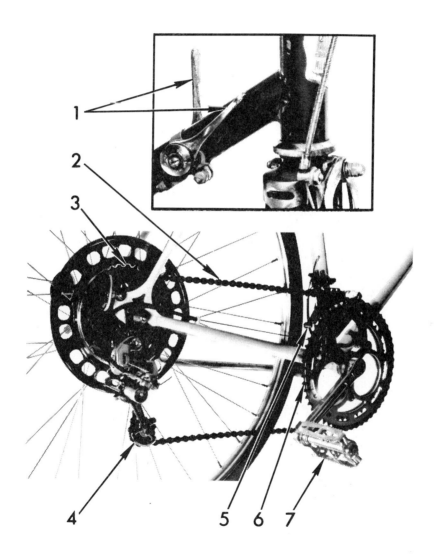

REMOVE AND INSTALL FRONT DERAILLEUR

Remove Front Derailleur.

1. Loosen nut or screw (11) in retainer (10). Disconnect cable (12) by pulling cable from retainer and boss (9).

2. Remove screw (7) by removing nut and washer. Remove spacer (8).

3. Remove bolt (5). Remove clamp (6) by removing nut or bolt (2) and washer. Remove derailleur (1).

REMOVE ENDS HERE

Install Front Derailleur.

4. Place and hold derailleur (1) at installed position. Loosely install clamp (6) by installing bolt (5), washer and nut (2).

Derailleur (1) is positioned so that front and rear of outer chain guide (3) is 1/16 – 1/8 inch above teeth on large chainwheel (4).

If chain guard is installed, position outer chain guide (3) until distance between chain guard and chain guide is 1/16—1/8 inch.

5. Position derailleur (1). Tighten nut or bolt (2) and bolt (5).

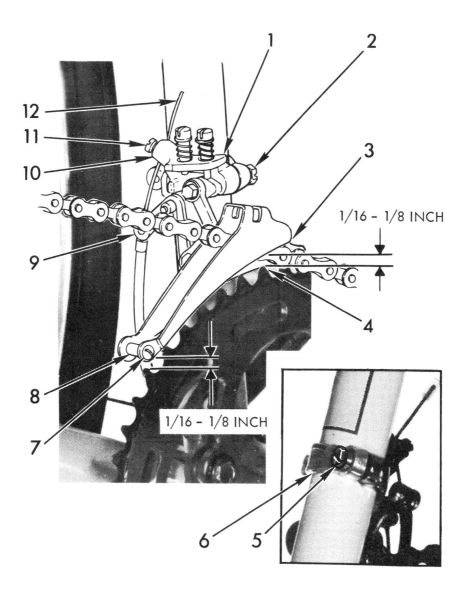

REMOVE AND INSTALL FRONT DERAILLEUR

If Suntour front derailleur is installed, chain must
be on large chainwheel (8).

1. Push selector lever (1) to full forward
    position.

2. Insert cable end (2) through boss (5)
    and retainer (4). Pull cable end until slack
    is removed. Tighten nut or screw (3).

3. Place spacer (6) at installed position.
    Install screw (7) by installing washer and nut.

4. Adjust front derailleur (Page 68).

   INSTALL ENDS HERE

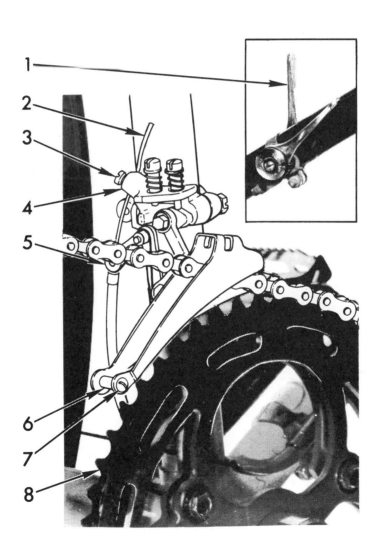

ADJUST FRONT DERAILLEUR

Rear wheel must be supported off ground.

While performing instructions in this section, selector levers (2,3) must be moved back and forth. If Suntour front derailleur is installed, lever (2) must be moved in opposite direction of following instructions.

1. While turning pedals, move levers (2,3) to full forward position. Turn pedals until chain (9) moves to small chainwheel (8) and smallest sprocket (1).

2. Check that speed selector cable (10) has no slack.

If cable has no slack, go to Step 4.

3. Loosen nut or screw (11). Remove slack in cable (10) by pulling cable end (12) until tight. Tighten nut or screw.

4. While turning pedals, move lever (2) to full rear position. Check that distance (6) between front and rear of outer chain guide (5) and teeth on large chainwheel (7) is 1/16 – 1/8 inch.

If distance (6) is 1/16 – 1/8 inch, go to Page 69, Step 1.

5. Loosen nut (4). Position chain guide (5) so that distance (6) is 1/16 – 1/8 inch. Tighten nut.

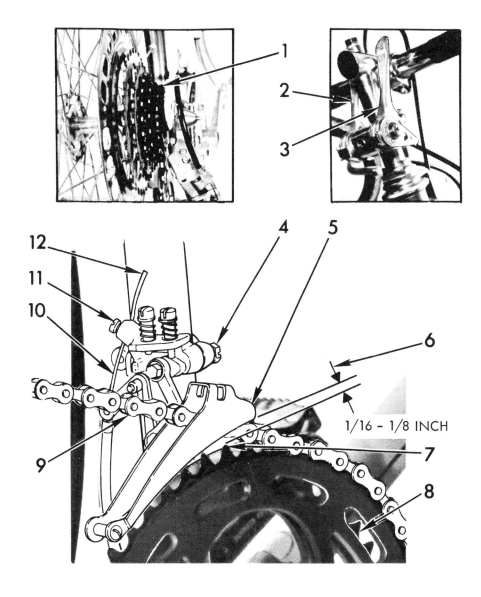

1/16 - 1/8 INCH

ADJUST FRONT DERAILLEUR

1. Check that chain guide (6) is aligned with chainwheel (5).

If chain guide (6) is aligned, go to Step 3.

2. Loosen clamp (4) by loosening nut or bolt (3). Align chain guide (6) with chainwheel (5). Tighten clamp.

3. While turning pedals, move lever (1) to full forward position. Turn pedals until chain (7) moves to small chainwheel (5).

If Huret derailleur is installed, go to Step 5.

4. Turn adjusting screw (2) until distance (8) between chain (7) and outer edge of chain guide (6) is 1/32 inch. Go to Page 70, Step 1.

5. Loosen nut or bolt (9). Move chain guide (6) until distance (8) between chain (7) and outer edge of chain guide (6) is 1/32 inch. Tighten nut or bolt.

"Go slow"

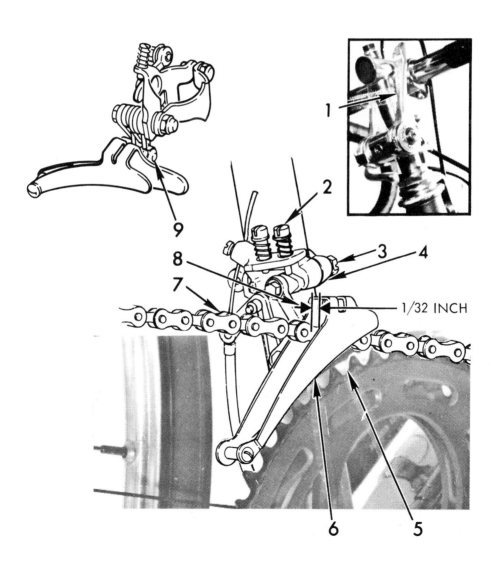

ADJUST FRONT DERAILLEUR

1. Turn high speed adjusting screw (8) counterclockwise three turns.

2. While turning pedals, move lever (1) to rear until distance (3) between chain (7) and inside edge of chain guide (6) is 1/32 inch.

3. Turn adjusting screw (8) clockwise until screw just touches derailleur arm (2). Back screw (8) off one turn.

4. While turning pedals, move lever (1) to full forward position. Move lever to full rear position. Check that chain (7) moves smoothly to large chainwheel (5).

If chain moves smoothly, go to Step 6.

5. Carefully bend front inside edge of chain guide (6) toward chain (7). Repeat Step 4.

6. While riding bicycle and operating lever (1), check that chain guide (6) moves chain (7) to large and small chainwheels (5,4) smoothly.

If chain does not move smoothly, go to Page 68, Step 1, to readjust front derailleur.

7. Adjust rear derailleur (Page 73).

ADJUST ENDS HERE

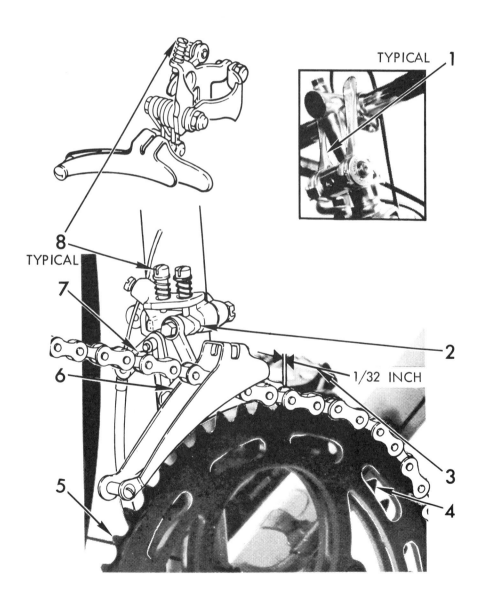

REMOVE AND INSTALL REAR DERAILLEUR

Rear wheel must be removed (Page 43).

On some derailleurs, it is necessary to remove the chain before removing the derailleur (Page 98).

Remove Rear Derailleur.

1. Push selector lever (9) to full forward position.

2. Remove cable cap (10), if installed. Loosen nut or screw in retainer (7). Remove speed selector cable (8).

3. Remove bolt (5) and nut, or screw (2). Remove derailleur (6).

REMOVE ENDS HERE

Install Rear Derailleur.

If derailleur (6) has elongated slot (1), derailleur must be installed with indicator line (3) parallel to chain stay (4).

4. Place and hold derailleur (6) at installed position. Install bolt (5) and nut, or screw (2).

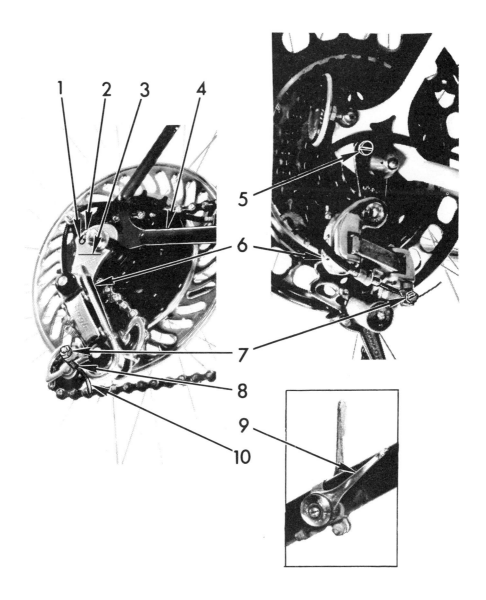

REMOVE AND INSTALL REAR DERAILLEUR

1.   Install cable (4) through retainer (2).

2.   Remove slack in cable (1) by pulling cable
     end (4). Tighten nut or screw (3).

3.   Install cable cap (5), if removed.

4.   Install chain, if removed (Page 98).

5.   Install rear wheel (Page 43).
     Adjust rear derailleur (Page 73).

INSTALL ENDS HERE

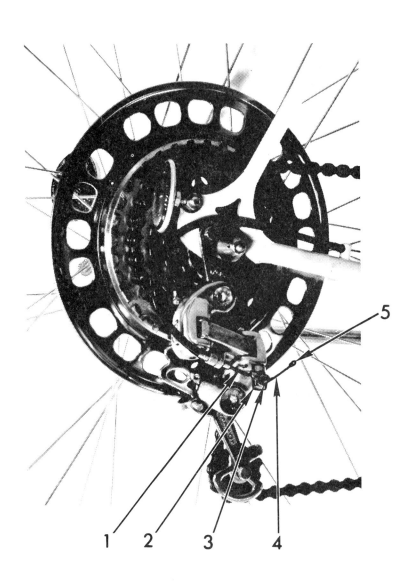

ADJUST REAR DERAILLEUR

Procedures in this section apply to Huret or
Sprint (1), Shimano (2), Simplex (4), Suntour (3),
and Campagnolo (5) rear derailleurs. (See also
page 74.)

Rear wheel must be supported off ground
to perform this section.

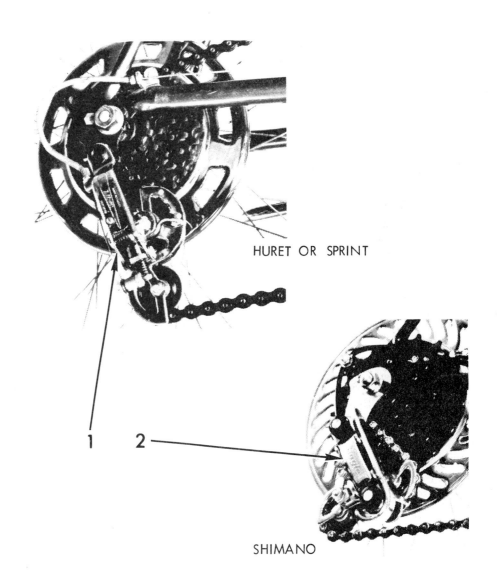

HURET OR SPRINT

1   2

SHIMANO

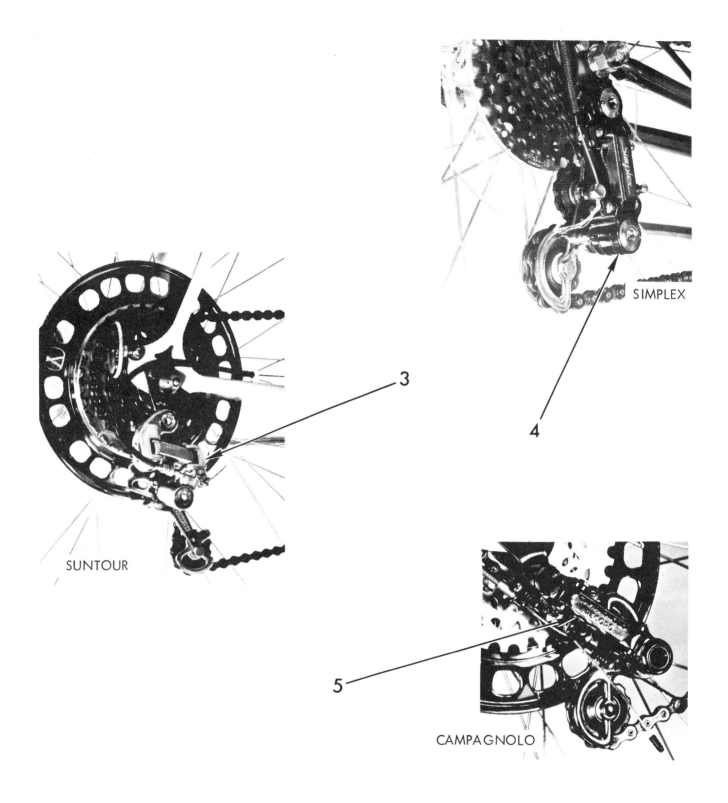

SIMPLEX

3

4

SUNTOUR

5

CAMPAGNOLO

ADJUST REAR DERAILLEUR

All.

1. While turning pedal, check that jockey wheel (4) tracks in center of chain (2).

If jockey wheel does not track in center of chain, go to Page 76, Step 1.

Middle sprocket must be aligned with centerline of chainwheel on 5 speed bicycles.

Middle sprocket must be aligned with centerline between chainwheels on 10 speed bicycles.

Middle sprocket must be aligned with centerline of middle chainwheel on 15 speed bicycles.

2. Check that middle sprocket (3) is aligned with centerline (1) of chainwheels.

If sprocket is aligned, go to Page 76, Step 4.

If sprocket is not aligned, bicycle must be taken to dealer.

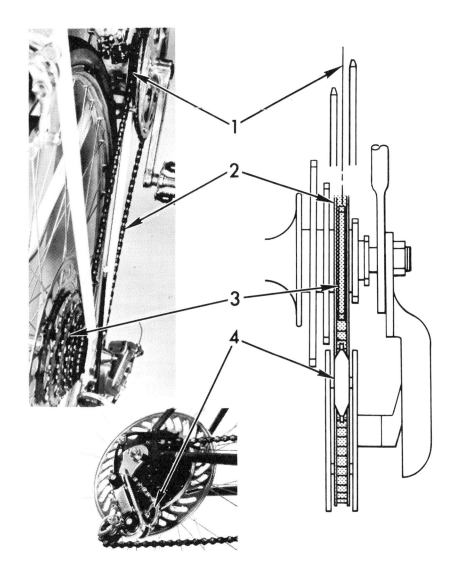

ADJUST REAR DERAILLEUR

All.

1. Check that mounting bracket (2) is not bent.

If not bent, go to Step 3.

2. Using adjustable wrench, straighten bracket (2).

3. Using adjustable wrench, carefully twist derailleur arm (4) until jockey wheel (3) is aligned with center of chain (5). Go to Page 75, Step 1.

4. While turning pedal forward, push right selector lever (1) forward.

5. Check that derailleur cable (6) has slight amount of slack.

If cable has slight amount of slack, go to Page 78, Step 6.

"Easy on the muscle."

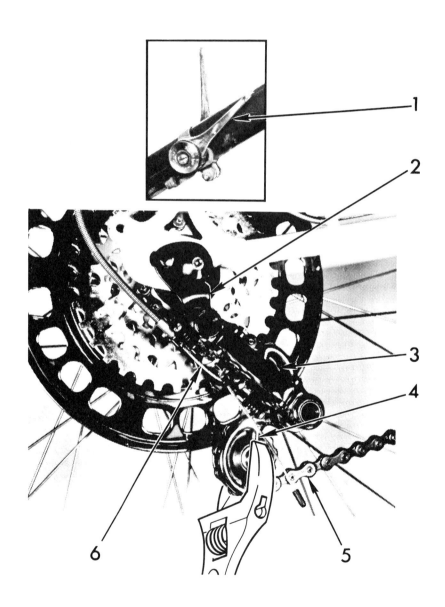

ADJUST REAR DERAILLEUR

__All.__

1. Check that cable adjusting barrel (4) has more than 1/8 inch of thread (3) showing through cable holder.

    If adjusting barrel has less than 1/8-inch thread showing, go to Page 78, Step 1.

2. Turn adjusting barrel (4) two turns counterclockwise.

3. While turning pedal forward, move right selector lever (1) full back, and then full forward.

4. Check that derailleur cable (2) has slight amount of slack.

    If cable does not have slight amount of slack, repeat Steps 2 through 4.

    If cable has slight amount of slack, go to Page 78, Step 6.

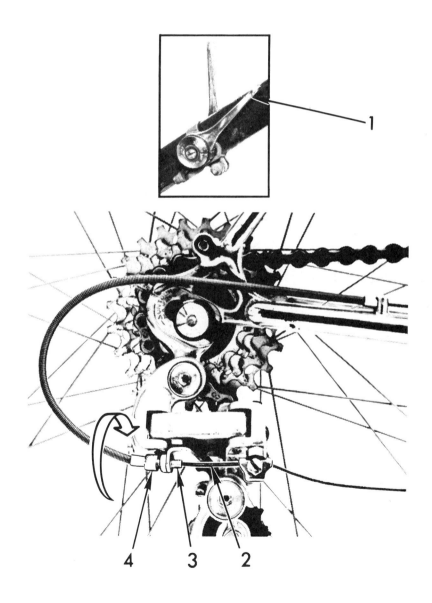

ADJUST REAR DERAILLEUR

1. Turn adjusting barrel (7) clockwise until maximum amount of thread shows through cable holder (6).

2. Loosen anchor bolt (4) and nut. Pull cable (5) tight.

3. While holding cable (5), tighten anchor bolt (4) and nut.

4. While turning pedal, move right selector lever (1) full back, and then full forward.

5. Check that cable (5) has slight amount of slack.

If cable does not have slight amount of slack, go to Page 77, Step 1.

6. While turning pedal, check that chain (2) stays on smallest sprocket (3).

If chain stays on smallest sprocket (3), go to Page 79, Step 2.

7. Carefully place chain (2) on smallest sprocket (3).

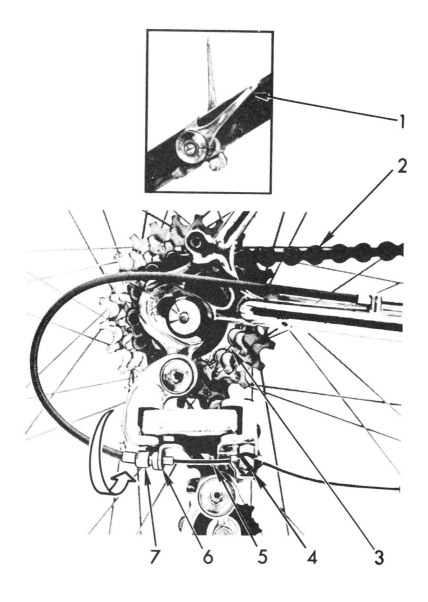

ADJUST REAR DERAILLEUR

All.

1. While turning pedal, turn high gear adjusting screw (5), see also page 80, clockwise or counterclockwise until chain (2) stays on smallest sprocket (3).

2. While turning pedal, pull right lever (1) back until chain (2) is on second smallest sprocket (4). Push right lever forward.

3. Check that chain (2) goes to smallest sprocket (3).

If chain is not on smallest sprocket, repeat Steps 1 through 3.

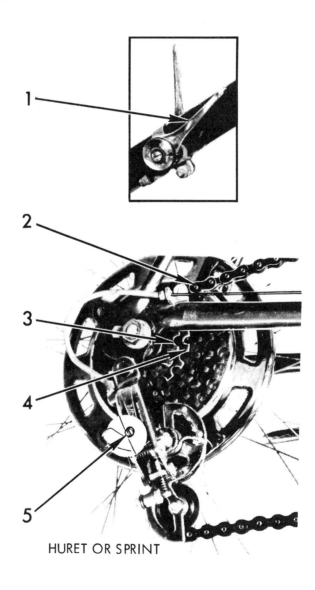

HURET OR SPRINT

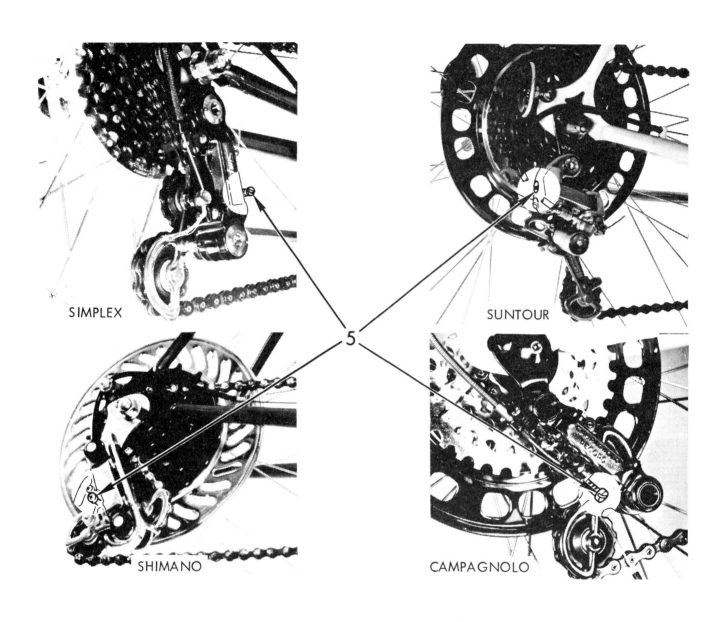

SIMPLEX

SUNTOUR

5

SHIMANO

CAMPAGNOLO

ADJUST REAR DERAILLEUR

All.

1. While turning pedal, pull right lever (1) full back. Check that chain (2) is on largest sprocket (3).

If chain is not on largest sprocket, go to Step 4.

2. While turning pedal, push right lever (1) forward until chain (2) goes to second largest sprocket (4). Pull lever back.

3. Check that chain (2) goes to largest sprocket (3).

If chain is on largest sprocket, go to Page 83, Step 1.

4. While turning pedal, turn low gear adjusting screw (5), see also Page 82, clockwise or counterclockwise until chain (2) stays on largest sprocket (3).

5. Repeat Steps 1 through 3.

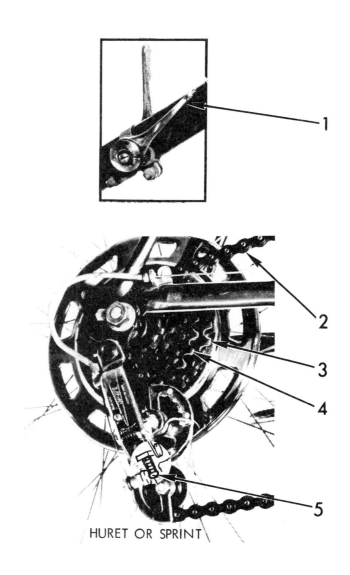

HURET OR SPRINT

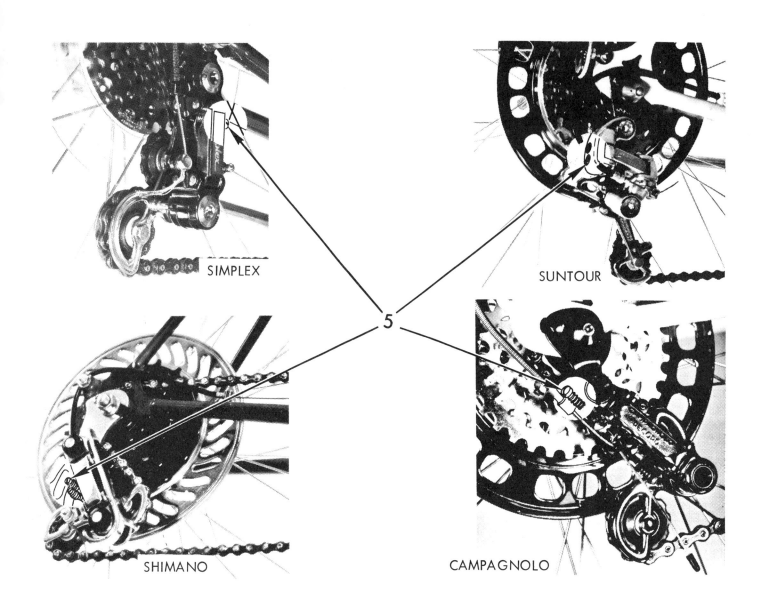

SIMPLEX

SUNTOUR

5

SHIMANO

CAMPAGNOLO

ADJUST REAR DERAILLEUR

All.

1. While turning pedal, push right lever (1) full forward. Check that chain (4) moves smoothly from largest sprocket (3) to smallest sprocket and does not slip.

If chain does not move smoothly, chain must be inspected (Page 96).

2. Check that sprocket teeth (2) are not worn, burred, missing or damaged.

If sprocket teeth are worn, burred, missing or damaged, freewheel mechanism must be replaced (Page 45).

ADJUST ENDS HERE

"That wasn't so hard."

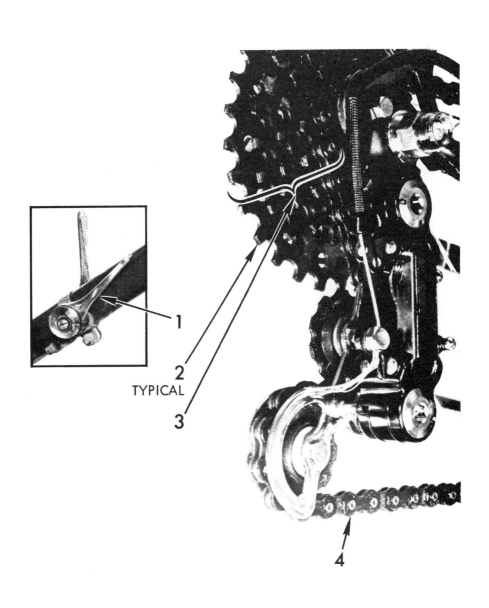

TYPICAL

REMOVE AND INSTALL SELECTOR LEVERS

Selector levers are fastened in several different ways. Levers may be installed at following locations:

Top tube (3)
Down tube (5)
Stem (2)
Handlebar tips (4)

If Huret (Sprint) or Suntour (1) levers are mounted on stem (2), stem must be removed (Page 10).

Speed selector cables must be removed (Page 92).

Remove Tube Mounted Selector Levers.

1. Remove screw (8) by removing nut (7). Remove selector levers (6).

REMOVE ENDS HERE

Install Tube Mounted Selector Levers.

2. Place selector levers (6) at installed position. Install screw (8) by installing nut (7).

3. Install speed selector cables (Page 93).

INSTALL ENDS HERE

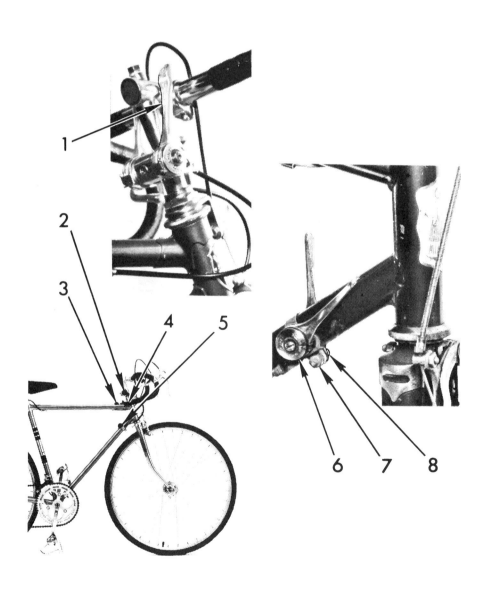

REMOVE AND INSTALL SELECTOR LEVERS

Remove Shimano Selector Levers.

1. Remove clamp (1) by removing bolts (2). Remove selector levers (3).

REMOVE ENDS HERE

Install Shimano Selector Levers.

2. Place selector levers (3) at installed position. Install clamp (1) by installing bolts (2).

3. Install speed selector cables (Page 93).

INSTALL ENDS HERE

Remove Huret (Sprint) Selector Levers.

4. Remove selector levers (4) by removing locknut (5) and washer.

REMOVE ENDS HERE

Install Huret (Sprint) Selector Levers.

5. Place selector levers (4) at installed position. Install washer and locknut (5).

6. Install stem (Page 10). Install speed selector cables (Page 93).

INSTALL ENDS HERE

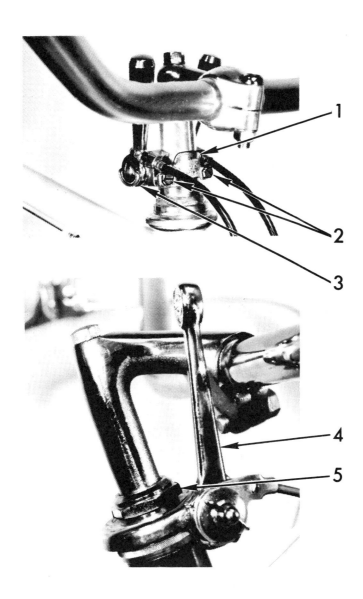

REMOVE AND INSTALL SELECTOR LEVERS

Remove Suntour Selector Levers.

1. Loosen clamp (2) by loosening screw (1). Remove selector levers (3).

REMOVE ENDS HERE

Install Suntour Selector Levers.

2. Place selector levers (3) at installed position. Tighten clamp (2) by tightening screw (1).

3. Install stem (Page 10). Install speed selector cables (Page 93).

INSTALL ENDS HERE

Remove Handlebar Tip Selector Levers.

4. Remove trim nut (7). Remove screw (5) by removing nut (6). Remove selector lever (8).

Allen screw is located inside selector body (4).

5. Using 6mm allen wrench, remove selector body (4).

REMOVE ENDS HERE

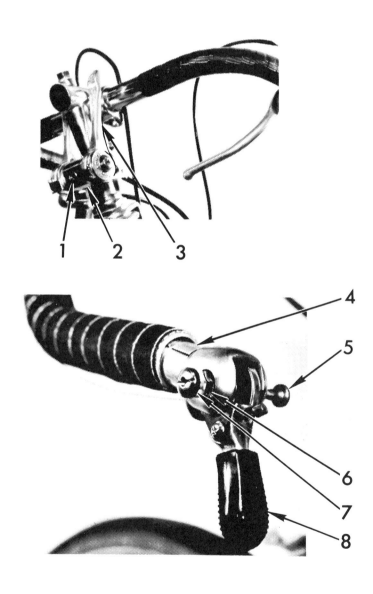

REMOVE AND INSTALL SELECTOR LEVERS

Install Handlebar Tip Selector Levers.

Selector body (4) is installed with manufacturer's identification facing up.

1. Install selector body (4) in handlebar tip (1). Using 6mm allen wrench, tighten body.

2. Align tab on selector lever (6) with slot in body (4). Install lever.

3. Install screw (5). Install nut (3). Install trim nut (2).

4. Install speed selector cables (Page 93).

   INSTALL ENDS HERE

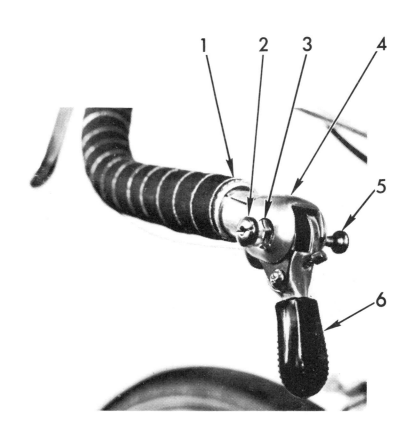

DISASSEMBLE AND ASSEMBLE SELECTOR LEVERS

Procedures in this section apply to left and right selector levers.

Following supplies will be required to perform instructions in this section:

Crocus cloth
Drycleaning solvent

Disassemble Selector Levers.

1. Loosen nut or screw in retainer (1 or 3).
    Disconnect speed selector cable (2) from retainer.

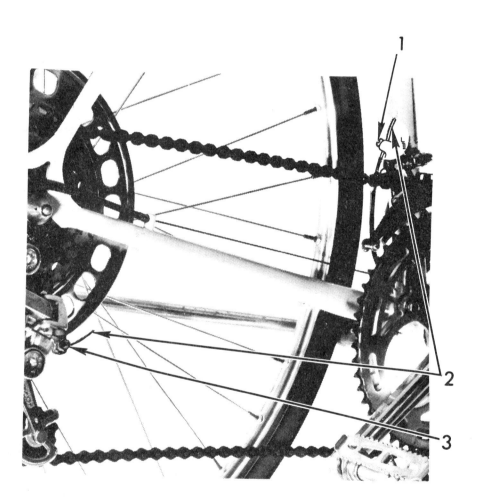

DISASSEMBLE AND ASSEMBLE SELECTOR LEVERS

Record order and position of selector lever parts for aid during assembly.

Steps presented apply to selector lever (3). The same steps apply to selector lever (1).

1. While holding selector lever (3), remove adjusting screw or bolt (8). Remove following parts:

   Pressure plate (7)
   Tension cup (6)
   Lever stop washer (5), if installed
   Selector lever (3)

2. Disconnect cable end (4) from selector lever (3).

3. Remove cable stop (2).

   DISASSEMBLE ENDS HERE

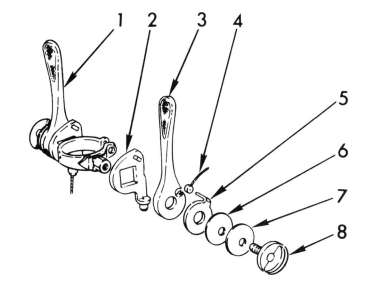

Assemble Selector Levers.

1. Using solvent, clean all parts.

Crocus cloth should be used to clean any rusted parts.

2. Check that following parts are not bent, cracked, or rusted:

   Pressure plate (6)
   Tension cup (5)
   Lever stop washer (4), if installed
   Cable stop (1)

3. Check that selector lever (2) is not bent or damaged.

4. Check that speed selector cable (3) is not frayed or worn.

5. Place and hold following parts on adjusting screw or bolt (7):

   Pressure plate (6)
   Tension cup (5)
   Lever stop washer (4), if removed.

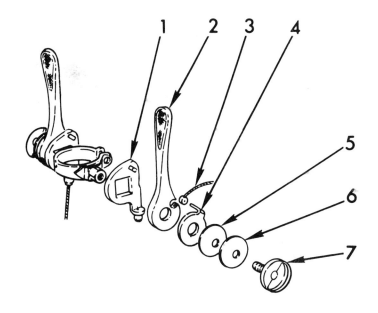

89

DISASSEMBLE AND ASSEMBLE SELECTOR LEVERS

1. Connect cable end (4) to selector lever (3).

2. Install selector lever (3) on adjusting screw or bolt (6).

3. Place cable stop (2) on bracket (1).

4. While holding adjusting screw or bolt (6) with assembled parts, align stop washer (5), if installed, with slot in cable stop (2).

5. Install adjusting screw or bolt (6) fingertight. Tighten one full turn.

Movement of selector levers (7) should be stiff but not difficult.

Adjustment screw or nut (8) is turned clockwise to stiffen movement of selector levers (7). Screw or nut is turned counterclockwise to loosen movement.

6. Adjust screw or nut (8) until movement of selector levers (7) is stiff but not difficult.

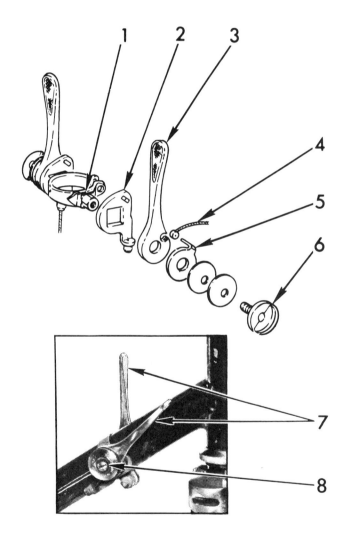

DISASSEMBLE AND ASSEMBLE SELECTOR LEVERS

1. Install speed selector cables (2) through retainers (1 or 3). Tighten nuts or screws.

2. Adjust derailleur (rear derailleur, Page 73, front derailleur, Page 68).

        ASSEMBLE ENDS HERE

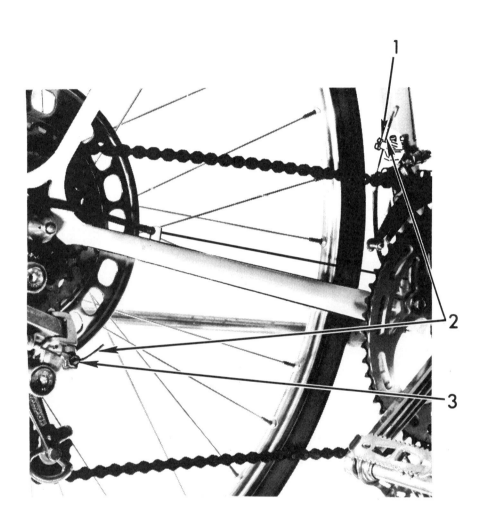

REMOVE AND INSTALL SPEED SELECTOR CABLES

Procedures in this section apply to front and rear speed selector cables.

Following supplies are required to perform instructions in this section:

Bicycle cable grease
Clean cloth

Rear wheel must be supported off ground.

While performing instructions in this section, selector levers (2,3) must be moved back and forth.

If removing Suntour front derailleur speed selector cable, chain must be on large chainwheel in Step 1.

Remove Speed Selector Cables.

1. While turning pedals, push selector levers (2,3) to full forward position until chain (6) is on smallest sprocket (8) and smallest chainwheel (5).

2. Loosen nut or screw in retainers (4,7).

3. Pull lever (2,3) to full rear position. Push lever to mid-range position.

4. Check that cable end (1) is loose in lever (2,3).

If cable is not loose in lever (2,3), selector lever must be disassembled before continuing (Page 88).

REMOVE AND INSTALL SPEED SELECTOR CABLES

1. Remove cable (5) by pulling through lever (4,7) and cable housing (2,6).

If cable housing (2,6) is not to be removed, **REMOVE ENDS HERE.**

Cable housing (2,6) is attached to bicycle by clamps, screws or inserted in a boss (3,8).

2. Remove cable housing (2,6) from boss (3,8).

REMOVE ENDS HERE

Install Speed Selector Cables.

If cable housing (2,6) has not been removed, go to Page 94, Step 1.

If installing new housing (2,6), housing must be cut to length using old housing as guide. Housing is cut between coils (1), using diagonal cutting pliers.

3. Cut housing (2,6) to correct length. Check that inside and outside edges of housing are not burred.

Cable housing (2,6) is attached to bicycle by clamps, screws or inserted in a boss (3,8).

4. Place housing (2,6) at installed position in boss (3,8).

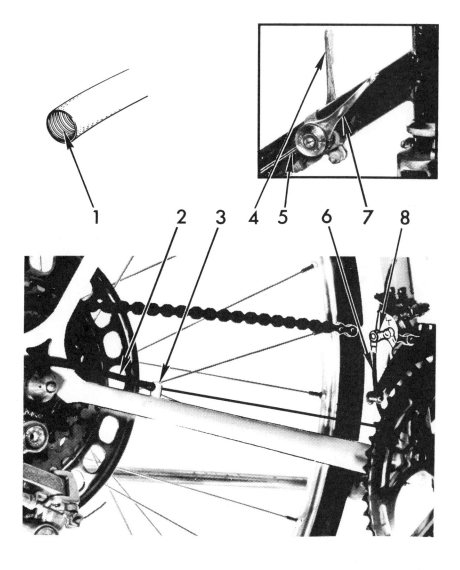

REMOVE AND INSTALL SPEED SELECTOR CABLES

1. Apply light coat of grease to speed selector cables (1).

2. Install cable end (6,8) through selector lever (2,3), housing (4,7), and through retainers (5,9).

If selector lever (2,3) has been disassembled, lever must be assembled before continuing (Page 88).

3. Push selector lever (2,3) to full forward position.

4. Pull cable end (6,8) until tight. Tighten nut or screw in retainers (5,9).

5. While turning pedal, move selector lever (2,3) back and forth several times. Wipe excess grease from cable end (6,8).

6. Adjust derailleur (rear derailleur, Page 73, front derailleur, Page 68).

INSTALL ENDS HERE

CRANK UNIT AND CHAIN

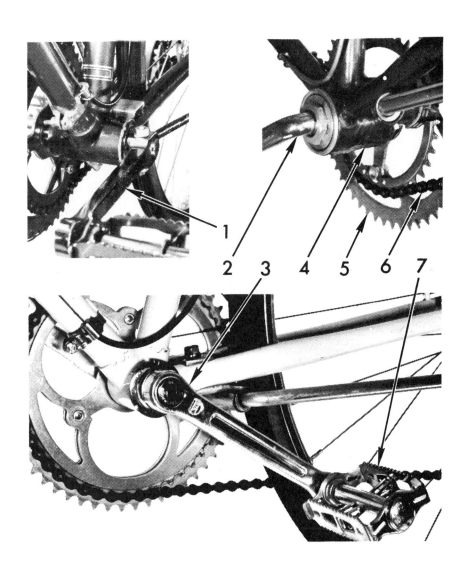

INSPECT CHAIN

Chain guard must be removed, if installed (Page 16).

Rear wheel must be supported.

Inspect Chain.

1. Check that chain (2) is not dry or dirty.

If dry or dirty, chain must be serviced (Page 103).

2. Check that chain side plates (3,5) and rollers (4) are not cracked or bent.

3. Slowly turn pedal. Check that chain does not jump or twist when going through front derailleur (6) or rear derailleur (1).

If links jump or twist, chain must be repaired (Page 100).

4. Install chain guard, if removed (Page 16).

INSPECT ENDS HERE

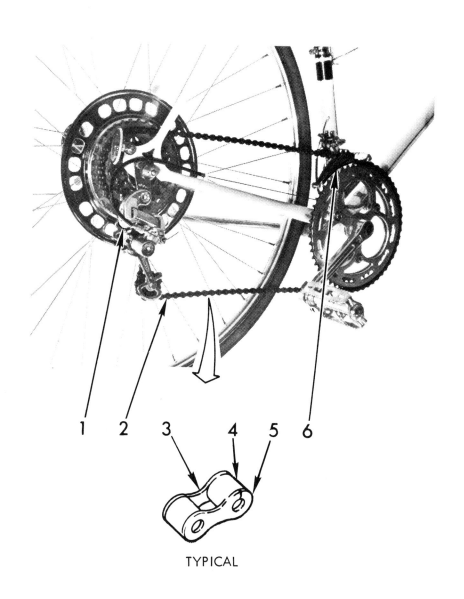

TYPICAL

DISCONNECT AND CONNECT CHAIN

Chain guard must be removed, if installed (Page 16).

Chain (1) must be on small chainwheel (2).

Disconnect Chain.

1. Disconnect chain (1) by pulling chain forward and over small chainwheel (2).

    DISCONNECT ENDS HERE

Connect Chain.

2. Pull chain (1) forward. Place chain on small chainwheel (2).

3. Install chain guard, if removed (Page 16).

    CONNECT ENDS HERE

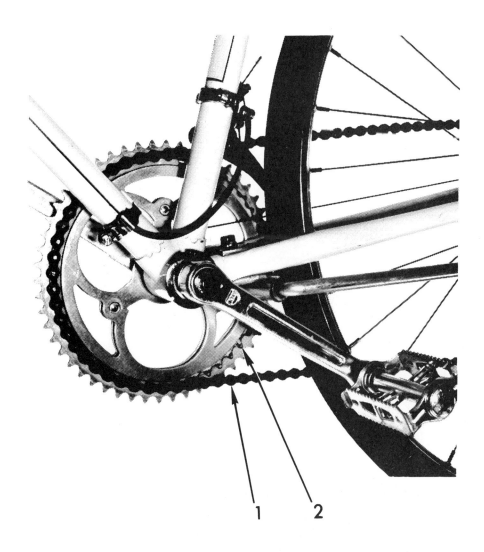

REMOVE AND INSTALL CHAIN

Chain guard must be removed, if installed (Page 16).

_____

The following tools will be needed to perform instructions in this section:

Chain tool (2) (see dealer for correct size)

Remove Chain.

1. Place link (3) over tab (4) of chain tool (2). Turn handle (1) clockwise until point (8) touches rivet (7).

CAUTION

For aid in installation, do not push rivet (7) all the way out of side plate (5). Turn handle (1) 1/2-turn at a time.

2. Line up rivet (7) with point (8). Turn handle (1) clockwise until rivet (7) is free of link (3).

3. Turn handle (1) counterclockwise until point (8) is free of chain (6). Remove chain (6) from tool (2).

4. Remove chain (6) from bike.

REMOVE ENDS HERE

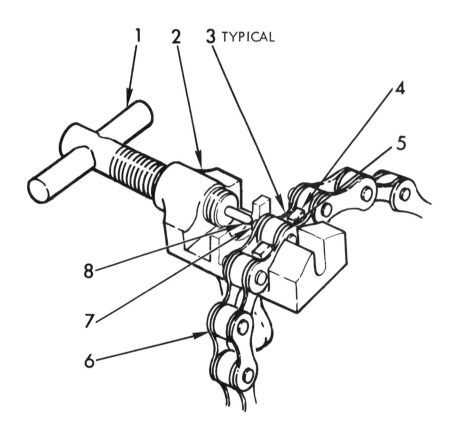

1   2   3 TYPICAL

98

REMOVE AND INSTALL CHAIN

Install Chain.

For aid in installation, use roller end of chain to thread chain.

1. Place end of chain (4) on smallest sprocket (3). Thread chain over jockey pulley (2) and around idler pulley (1).

2. Pull chain (4) around small chainwheel (9) and through front derailleur (8).

3. Place link (6) over tab (7). Line up side plates (10) and rivet (5) with hole in link (6).

4. Line up point (11) with rivet (5). Turn handle (13) clockwise until point touches rivet.

CAUTION

Be sure link (6) is straight in chain tool (12). Be sure rivet (5) extends same distance from both side plates (10).

5. Turn handle (13) clockwise until rivet (5) is pressed through side plates (10).

6. Turn handle (13) counterclockwise. Remove chain tool (12).

7. Install chain guard, if removed (Page 16).

INSTALL ENDS HERE

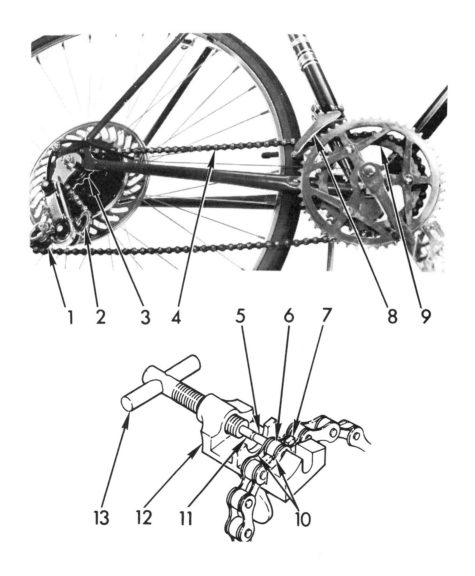

99

REPAIR CHAIN

Following tools and supplies will be needed to perform instructions in this section:

Chain tool (3) (see dealer for correct size)
Penetrating oil
Clean cloth

Chain must be removed (Page 98).

Repair Tight Links.

1. Apply penetrating oil to link (1). Twist and bend link five times. Check that link moves freely.

If all links (1) move freely, install chain (Page 99).

2. Check that side plates (6,7) of link (1) are not bent.

If side plates (6,7) are bent, replace link (Page 101, Step 5).

3. Rotate chain tool handle (2) counterclockwise. Place link (1) over tab (8).

4. Turn handle (2) clockwise until point (4) touches rivet (5).

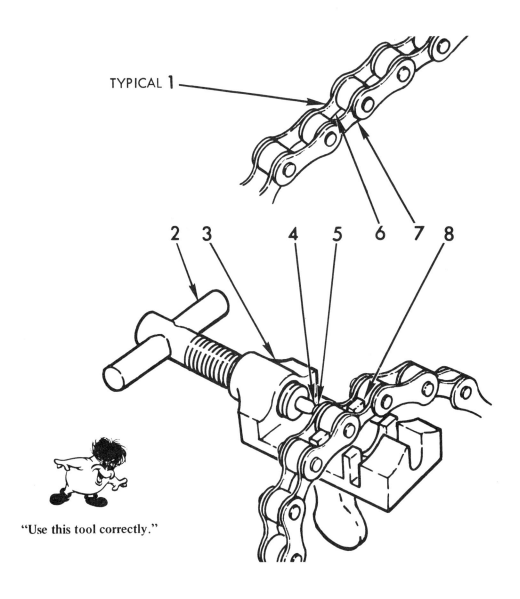

TYPICAL 1

2 3 4 5 6 7 8

"Use this tool correctly."

REPAIR CHAIN

CAUTION

Link (3) must be straight in slot (4). Rivet (2) should be slightly extended from both side plates (13,14).

1.   Turn handle (1) 1/4–turn clockwise. Turn handle counterclockwise.

2.   Check that link (3) moves freely.

If all links (3) move freely, go to Step 4.

3.   Repeat Page 100, Step 3 and 4, and Page 101, Step 1 and 2.

4.   Install chain (Page 99).

REPAIR ENDS HERE

Replace Links.

5.   Place link (6) over tab (8). Turn handle (12) clockwise until point (11) touches rivet (10).

CAUTION

For aid in installation, do not push rivet (10) all the way out of side plate (9). Turn handle (12) 1/2-turn at a time.

6.   Line up rivet (10) with point (11). Turn handle (12) clockwise until rivet (10) is free of link (5).

7.   Turn handle (12) counterclockwise until point (11) is free of chain. Repeat Step 5 through 7 for other rivet (7) in link (6).

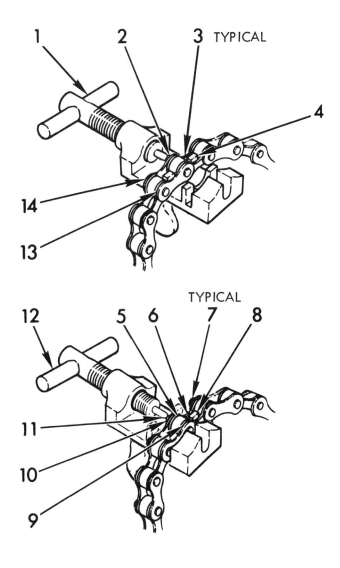

REPAIR CHAIN

1. Remove chain (4) from tool. Twist chain until link (7) is separated. Remove link.

2. Place chain (4) over tab (9) with rivet (1) toward handle (10).

3. Place new link (7) over tab (8). Line up link with rivet (1).

Rivet (1) should extend same distance from both side plates (2,3) when installed.

4. Turn handle (10) clockwise until rivet (1) is driven through side plate (3).

5. Remove chain (4) from tool.

6. Place chain (5) around large chainwheel (6) with new link at top of chainwheel. Hold chain at bottom of chainwheel. Pull up at top of chain.

If chain (5) can be removed from chainwheel (6), chain must be replaced.

7. Install chain (Page 99).

REPLACE ENDS HERE

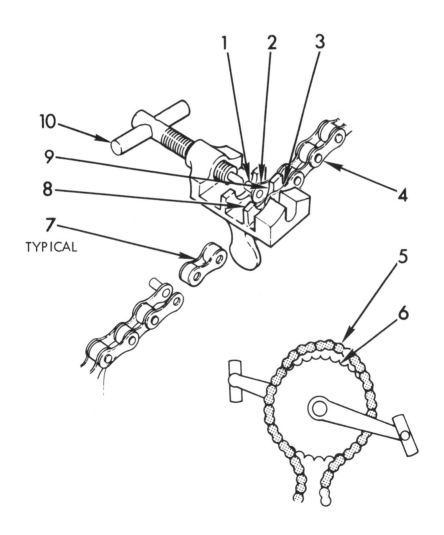

TYPICAL

SERVICE CHAIN

Chain guard must be removed, if installed (Page 16). Rear wheel must be supported.

Following supplies will be needed to perform instructions in this section:

Chain lubricant or 20 weight oil
Drycleaning solvent
Small bristle brush
Clean cloth

1. Check that chain (1) is not corroded or rusted.

If chain (1) is corroded or rusted, go to Step 3.

2. Using clean cloth dampened with solvent, wipe chain (1). Wipe chain dry. Go to Step 4.

3. Using brush and solvent, clean chain (1). Wipe chain dry.

4. While slowly turning pedal (2), lightly apply lubricant or oil to chain (1). Wipe excess oil from chain.

5. Install chain guard, if removed (Page 16).

SERVICE ENDS HERE

1   2

REMOVE AND INSTALL COTTERED CRANK AND CHAINWHEEL

Procedures in this section apply to left and right crank.

If removing right crank and chainwheel, chain must be disconnected (Page 97).

Remove Cottered Crank and Chainwheel.

If removing chainwheel only, go to Step 4.

1.   Remove nut (4) and washer. Position crank (3) until threaded end of cotter (5) is straight up.

CAUTION

Crank (3) must be firmly supported when removing cotter (5). Block of wood may be used.

Cotter (5) must be hit sharply. **If hit lightly, cotter may bend.**

2.   While supporting crank (3), sharply hit threaded end of cotter (5) downward. Remove cotter.

3.   Remove crank (3).

If removing cottered crank only, **REMOVE ENDS HERE.**

4.   Remove chainwheel (1) by removing bolts (2).

REMOVE ENDS HERE

REMOVE AND INSTALL COTTERED CRANK AND CHAINWHEELS

Install Cottered Crank and Chainwheels.

If installing chainwheels only, go to Step 6.

1. Check that cotter (5) is not bent or worn.

Flat side in spindle (6) must be forward.
Crank (3) must point forward.

2. Push crank (3) on spindle (6).

3. Press cotter (5) through hole of crank (3) and spindle (6) fingertight. Check that threads on cotter extend more than 1/4 inch.

If threads extend more than 1/4 inch, go to Step 5. Read information preceding Step.

4. Remove cotter (5). Using file, lightly file flat side of cotter. Repeat Step 3.

<u>CAUTION</u>

Do not overtighten nut (4).

Crank (3) must be firmly supported when tightening cotter (5).

5. While supporting crank (3), hit end of cotter (5). Install washer and nut (4).

6. Place chainwheels (1) at installed position. Install bolts (2).

7. Connect chain, if disconnected (Page 97).

INSTALL ENDS HERE

1 2 3 4 5 6

REMOVE AND INSTALL ONE-PIECE CRANK AND CHAINWHEELS

Following supplies will be needed to perform instructions in this section:

Bicycle grease
Drycleaning solvent
Clean cloth

Left pedal must be removed (Page 111).
Chain must be disconnected (Page 97).

Remove One-Piece Crank and Chainwheels.

1. Remove locknut (1) by turning clockwise. Remove keyed washer (2) from crank arm (4). Using screwdriver, remove adjustable cone (3) by turning counterclockwise.

2. Remove bearings (6) from arm (4). Slide arm (4) through bottom bracket (7) until right side bearings (10) can be seen.

3. Using screwdriver, carefully remove bearings (10) from cup (11). Remove crank (4) and chainwheels (8) from bracket (7).

4. Remove bearings (10) from arm (4). Remove cone (9) by turning clockwise. Remove washer, if installed.

5. Using hammer and punch, carefully remove cups (5,11).

REMOVE ENDS HERE

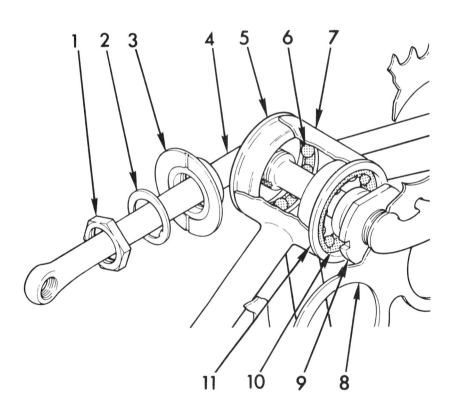

Install One-Piece Crank and Chainwheels.

1. Using solvent, clean all parts. Wipe dry with clean cloth.

2. Check that bearings (6,10) are not worn or pitted. Check that all parts are not worn or damaged.

3. Using hammer, carefully install cups (5,11) evenly in bottom bracket (7).

4. Place chainwheels (8) on crank (4). Install washer, if removed. Install cone (9) by turning counterclockwise.

5. Apply grease to bearings (6,10) and cups (5,11). Install right side bearings (10).

6. Place crank arm (4) through bottom bracket (7). Place and hold chainwheels (8) against bracket. Place bearings (6) in cup (5).

7. Install adjustable cone (3) by turning clockwise until tight. Install keyed washer (2). Install locknut (1) by turning counterclockwise.

8. Install pedal (Page 111). Adjust bottom bracket (Page 118).

INSTALL ENDS HERE

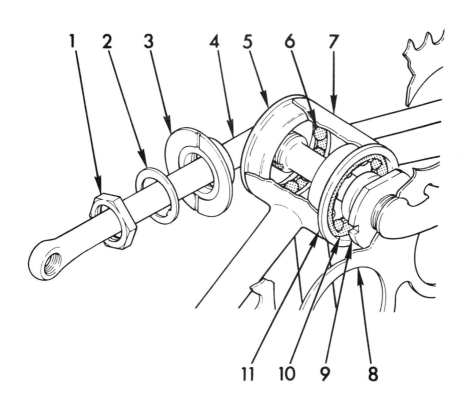

REMOVE AND INSTALL COTTERLESS CRANK AND CHAINWHEELS

Procedures in this section apply to left and right cotterless crank.

If removing cotterless crank only, the following tools and supplies will be needed to perform instructions in this section:

Cotterless crank extractor (see your dealer for
    correct size. Manufacturer of crank must
    be known)
Cotterless crank socket (see your dealer for
    correct size)
Bicycle oil
Clean cloth

Chain must be disconnected (Page 97).

Remove Cotterless Crank and Chainwheels.

1.   Remove dust cap (1) by turning cap counterclockwise.

2.   Using cotterless crank socket (5), remove bolt (3) by turning counterclockwise. Remove washer.

3.   Using clean cloth, clean threads of crank (2) and threads of crank extractor tool (4).

4.   Carefully install extractor tool (4) fingertight.

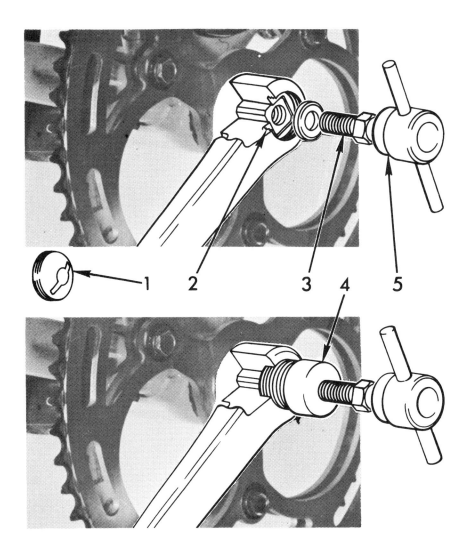

REMOVE AND INSTALL COTTERLESS CRANK AND CHAINWHEELS

Crank arm (7) must be held during next step.

1. Using crank socket (5), turn extractor (6) clockwise until crank (7) is loose.

If crank (7) does not come loose, remove crank socket (5) and lightly tap extractor (6). Repeat Step 1.

2. Remove crank (7). Remove extractor (6).

If removing cotterless crank only, **REMOVE ENDS HERE.**

Some chainwheels are secured with allen screws and nuts.

3. While holding chainwheels (4), remove bolts (3), spacer (2) and nuts (1). Remove chainwheels (4).

REMOVE ENDS HERE

Install Cotterless Crank and Chainwheels.

If installing crank only, go to Page 110, Step 1.

4. Place chainwheels (4) at installed position. Install bolts (3), spacers (2) and nuts (1).

5. Connect chain (Page 97).

INSTALL ENDS HERE

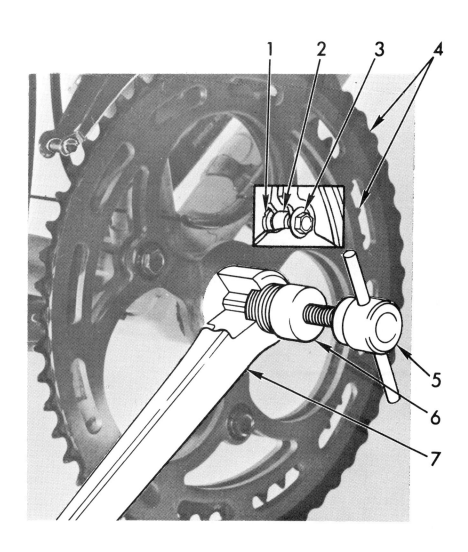

REMOVE AND INSTALL COTTERLESS CRANK AND CHAINWHEELS

If not installing new crank, go to Step 2.

1. Remove dust cap (1) by turning cap counter-clockwise. Go to Step 4.

2. Using clean cloth, clean spindle (2) and crank threads (3).

3. Apply light coat of oil to following:

    Spindle (2)
    Crank threads (3)
    Bolt (5)

4. Install crank arm (6). Install bolt (5) and washer fingertight.

CAUTION

Do not overtighten bolt (5).

5. Using crank socket (4), tighten bolt (5).

6. Install dust cap (1).

7. Connect chain, if disconnected (Page 97).

CAUTION

Bolt (5) must be retightened every 50 miles for first 150 miles.

INSTALL ENDS HERE

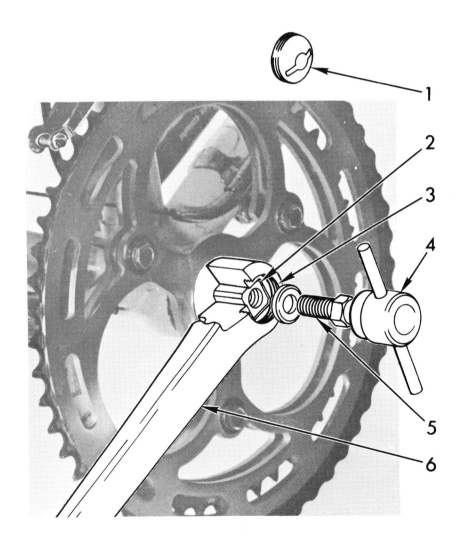

INSPECT PEDAL

Procedures in this section apply to adjustable and nonadjustable pedals. Dust cap (1) is installed on adjustable pedal.

Inspect Pedal.

1. Check that pedal (2) is not bent or damaged.

2. Check that spindle (3) is not bent or damaged.

3. Check that pedal (2) is mounted securely.

4. Slowly rotate pedal (2). Check that pedal turns freely without side play.

If pedal turns freely without side play, **INSPECT ENDS HERE.**

5. Replace nonadjustable pedal, if installed (Page 111).

6. Remove dust cap (1). Check that pedal (2) is greased and free of dirt.

If not, pedal must be overhauled (Page 113).

7. Adjust pedal (Page 112).

INSPECT ENDS HERE

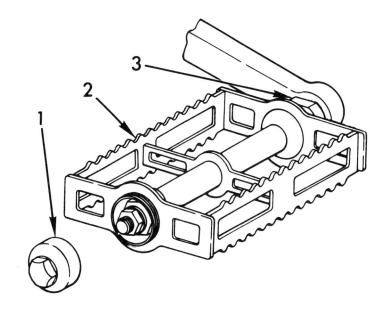

REMOVE AND INSTALL PEDAL

Remove Pedal.

1. Remove left pedal (1) by turning spindle (2) clockwise.

2. Remove right pedal (1) by turning spindle (2) counterclockwise.

REMOVE ENDS HERE

Install Pedal.

CAUTION

Left and right pedals (1) are stamped L or R on flat of spindle (2) or threaded end (3).

Do not force threads of spindle (2) into crank (4). Threads (3) may be damaged.

3. Install left pedal (1) by turning spindle (2) counterclockwise.

4. Install right pedal (1) by turning spindle (2) clockwise.

INSTALL ENDS HERE

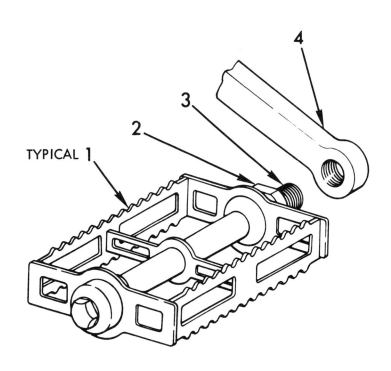

ADJUST PEDAL

Procedures in this section apply to adjustable pedals. Adjustable pedal has dust cap (1).

1. Remove dust cap (1). Loosen locknut (2). Tighten cone (3) hand tight by turning clockwise. Loosen cone 1/4-turn counterclockwise.

2. While holding cone (3), tighten locknut (2).

3. Slowly rotate pedal (4). Check that pedal turns freely and without side play.

If pedal turns freely and without side play, install dust cap (1).

ADJUST ENDS HERE

If pedal has side play, cone must be turned clockwise. If pedal will not turn freely, cone must be turned counterclockwise.

4. Adjust pedal (4). Go to Step 2.

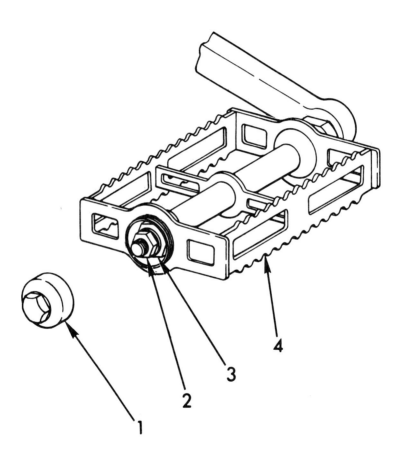

OVERHAUL PEDAL

Procedures in this section apply to left and right adjustable pedals.

The following supplies will be needed to perform instructions in this section:

Drycleaning solvent
Bicycle grease
Container
Stiff brush
Clean cloth
Tweezers

Pedal must be removed (Page 111).

1. Remove dust cap (1). While holding spindle (5), remove locknut (2). Remove keyed washer (3).

Observe and record number of bearings (6,7) removed for aid during installation.

2. Place container under pedal (8). Remove cone (4) and bearings (7).

3. Remove spindle (5) and bearings (6).

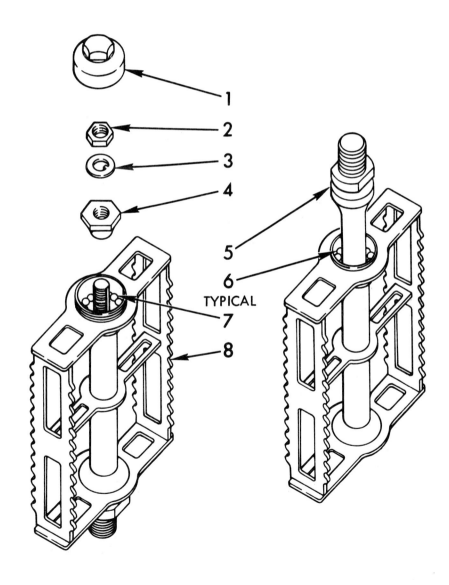

TYPICAL

OVERHAUL PEDAL

1. Using solvent with brush, clean following components:

   Locknut (1)
   Keyed washer (2)
   Cone (3)

2. Using solvent with brush, clean following components:

   Bearings (6,7)
   Spindle (4)
   Pedal (8)

3. Using clean cloth, dry following components:

   Locknut (1)
   Keyed washer (2)
   Cone (3)
   Bearings (6,7)
   Spindle (4)
   Pedal (8)

4. Check that bearings (6,7) are not dull, pitted, corroded or damaged.

5. Check that spindle (4) does not have damaged threads. Check that spindle is not bent or damaged.

6. Check that cone (3) is not pitted or damaged.

7. Apply thin coat of grease to races (5). Insert spindle (4) approximately 2 inches into pedal (8).

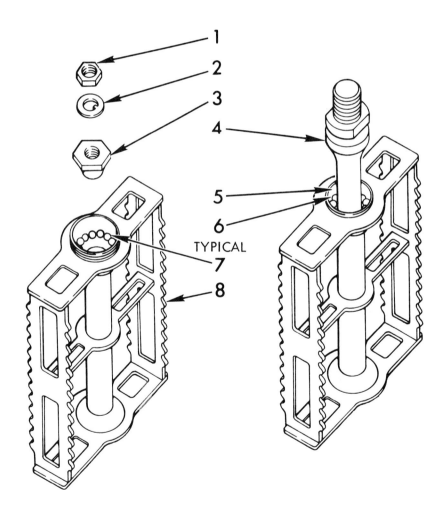

TYPICAL

OVERHAUL PEDAL

1. While holding pedal (9) and spindle (6), install bearings (7) using tweezers.

Too many bearings are identified by bearings touching. Too few bearings are identified by large gaps between bearings.

2. Check that bearings (7) are evenly spaced.

3. Apply thin coat of grease over bearings (7). Install spindle (6) fully into pedal (9).

4. While holding pedal (9) and spindle (6), turn pedal over.

5. Using tweezers, place bearings (8) in race (5).

6. Apply light coat of grease over bearings (8). Install cone (4) fingertight. Install keyed washer (3). Install locknut (2).

7. Adjust pedal (Page 112).

8. Install pedal (Page 111).

OVERHAUL ENDS HERE

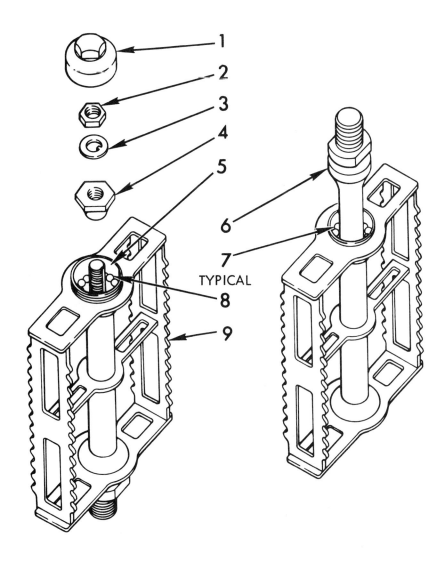

TYPICAL

INSPECT CHAINWHEEL

Chain must be disconnected (Page 97).

1. While turning chainwheel (2) slowly, check that teeth (1) are in line with chainwheel.

If teeth (1) are in line, go to Step 3.

CAUTION

Apply even pressure. Do not force teeth (1) when bending.

2. Using adjustable wrench, carefully bend teeth (1) until teeth are in line with chainwheel (2). Repeat Step 1.

3. Check that teeth (1) are not worn or broken.

If chainwheel (2) is worn or broken, it must be replaced. See section entitled Remove One-Piece Crank (Page 106), Cottered Crank (Page 104) or Cotterless Crank (Page 108).

4. Check that chainwheel (2) is not bent.

If bent, chainwheel must be taken to dealer for straightening.

5. Connect chain (Page 97).

INSPECT ENDS HERE

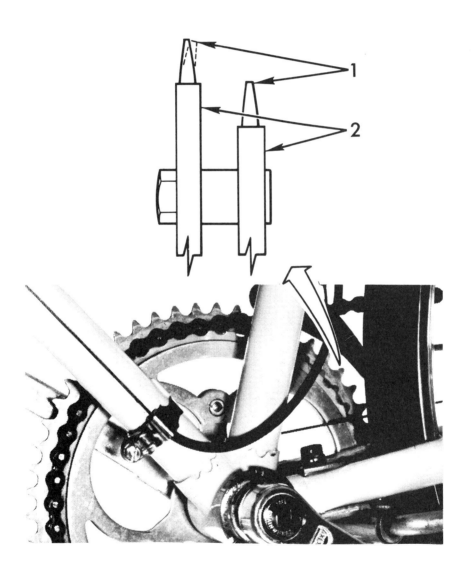

INSPECT CRANK

Procedures in this section apply to cottered crank (2), one-piece crank (1) and cotterless crank (3).

1. Slowly turn crank (1,2,3). Check that crank turns smoothly.

If crank (1,2,3) does not turn smoothly, bottom bracket must be adjusted (Page 118).

2. Slowly turn crank (1,2,3). Check that crank does not squeak or grind.

If crank (1,2,3) squeaks or grinds, crank must be overhauled. If one-piece crank is installed, see section entitled Remove and Install One-Piece Crank and Chainwheel (Page 106). If cottered crank or cotterless crank is installed, see section entitled Overhaul Bottom Bracket (Page 120).

3. Push and pull on crank (1,2,3). Check that crank is not loose.

If crank is loose, bottom bracket must be adjusted (Page 118).

4. Check that crank (1,2,3) is not broken or bent.

INSPECT ENDS HERE

117

ADJUST BOTTOM BRACKET

Procedures in this section apply to one-piece, cottered or cotterless cranks.

Chain must be disconnected (Page 97).

Proper adjustment of bottom bracket is achieved when spindle turns freely, and has no excessive end play. A small amount of end play is acceptable.

1. Slide spindle (5) in and out. Check that spindle has no excessive end play.

If spindle does not have excessive end play, go to Page 119, Step 1.

2. Loosen lock ring (3) by turning counter-clockwise or loosen locknut (1) by turning clockwise.

3. Turn cup (4) clockwise until spindle has no excessive end play or turn cup (2) counter-clockwise until spindle has no excessive end play.

4. Tighten lock ring (3) by turning clockwise or tighten locknut (1) by turning counterclockwise.

"Was that clockwise or counterclockwise?"

1 2   3   4   5

ADJUST BOTTOM BRACKET

1. Turn crank arm (4). Check that spindle (6) turns freely.

If spindle turns freely, go to Step 6.

2. Loosen lock ring (3) by turning counter-clockwise or loosen locknut (1) by turning clockwise.

3. Turn cup (5) 1/8-turn counterclockwise or turn cup (2) 1/8-turn clockwise.

4. Tighten lock ring (3) by turning clockwise or tighten locknut (1) by turning counterclockwise.

5. Turn crank arm (4). Check that spindle (6) turns freely.

If spindle (6) does not turn freely, repeat Steps 2 through 5.

6. Connect chain (Page 97).

ADJUST ENDS HERE

OVERHAUL BOTTOM BRACKET

Procedures in this section apply to bottom brackets that have cottered cranks or cotterless cranks.

Left and right cranks must be removed (cottered cranks, Page 104, cotterless cranks, Page 108).

Bicycle should be placed and supported on right side to perform instructions in this section.

The following supplies will be needed to perform instructions in this section:

Drycleaning solvent
Clean cloth
Bicycle grease

1. Remove lock ring (5) by turning counterclockwise.

2. Remove adjustable cup (6) by turning counterclockwise.

3. Remove loose bearings (4), if installed. Record number of bearings for aid during installation.

Note position of bearings (3,8) when removing for aid during installation.

4. Remove retained bearings (3), if installed. Remove spindle (2).

5. Remove stationary cup (1) by turning clockwise.

6. Remove loose bearings (7), if installed. Record number of bearings for aid during installation.

7. Remove retained bearings (8), if installed.

1. Using drycleaning solvent, clean all parts. Clean inside of bracket (1).

2. Using cloth, dry all parts. Dry inside of bracket (1).

Cracks, pits, or shiny spots indicate excessive wear.

3. Check that following parts do not show signs of excessive wear or rust:

    Stationary cup (2)
    Adjustable cup (6)
    Spindle (3)
    Bearings (4,7)
    Lock ring (5)

4. Apply small amount of bicycle grease to inside of stationary cup (2).

If loose bearings (7) were removed, go to Step 6.

5. Apply bicycle grease to retained bearings (8). Install retained bearings in stationary cup (2). Go to Page 121, Step 1.

6. Place bearings (7) in stationary cup (2). Apply small amount of bicycle grease to bearings. Go to Page 121, Step 2.

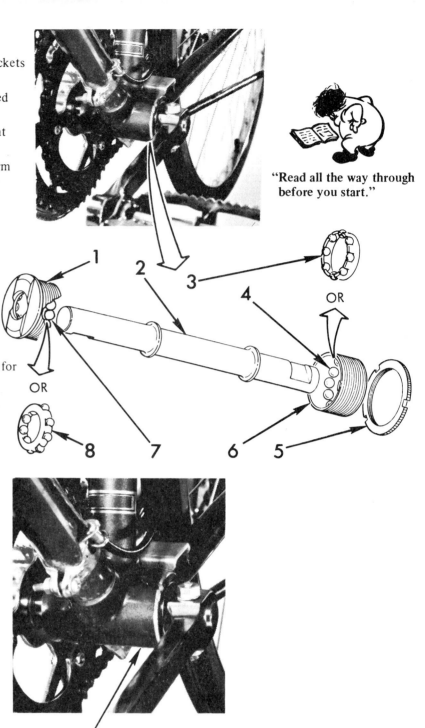

"Read all the way through before you start."

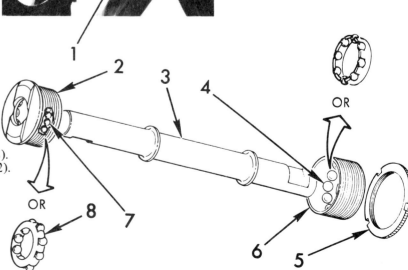

OVERHAUL BOTTOM BRACKET

1. Apply bicycle grease to retained bearings (5). Install retained bearings in adjustable cup (7). Go to Step 3.

2. Place bearings (6) in adjustable cup (7). Apply small amount of bicycle grease to bearings.

Distance from race (4) to end of spindle (2) is different on each end of spindle. Spindle is installed with longest distance toward chainwheel side of bracket (3).

3. Place stationary cup (1) on spindle (2). Install spindle.

4. Rotate stationary cup (1) counterclockwise to tighten.

CAUTION

Be sure bearings (5 or 6) do not fall out of adjustable cup (4) when installing cup.

5. Install adjustable cup (7) by turning clockwise. Install lock ring (8) by turning clockwise.

6. Adjust bottom bracket (3) (Page 118). Install left and right cranks (cottered cranks, Page 105, cotterless cranks, Page 109).

OVERHAUL ENDS HERE

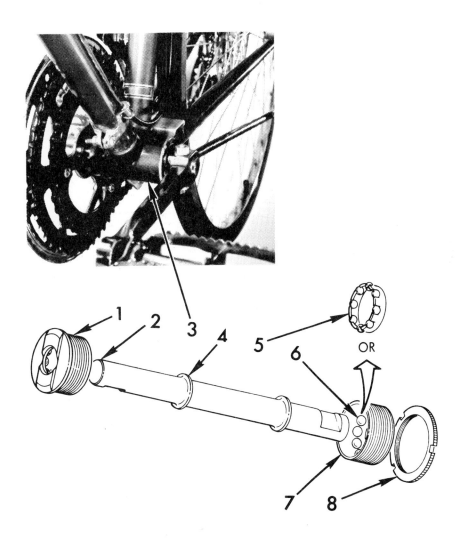

CONSTRUCT MAINTENANCE RACK

Following supplies will be required to construct bicycle rack:

Top Braces (2):

Two pieces of wood (prefer 1 inch X 4 inch)
Length: 10 inches + stem to handlebar distance (4)

Support Braces (5):

Two pieces of wood (prefer 1 inch X 3 inch)

Attaching Hardware (1):

Six nut (wing nut) and bolt combinations

Option: Nails may be used if rack is not to be folded up.

Bicycle Clamps (7,9):

Two electrical conduit clamps, to fit over top
  tube (6) or frame (11)
Two threaded stud and wing nut
  combinations (8,10)

Rack Supports (3):

Garage studs or substitute

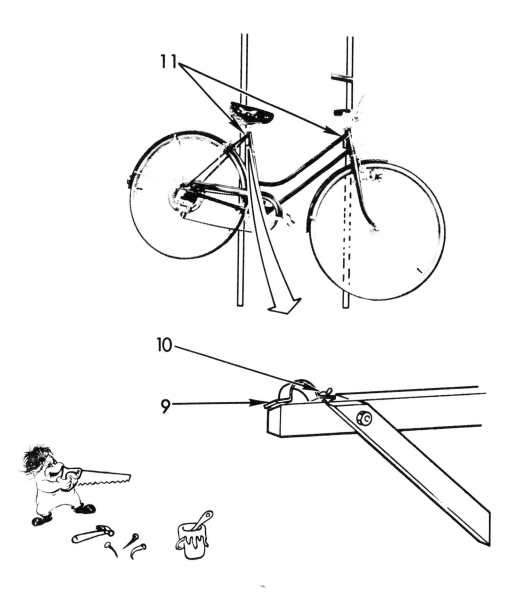

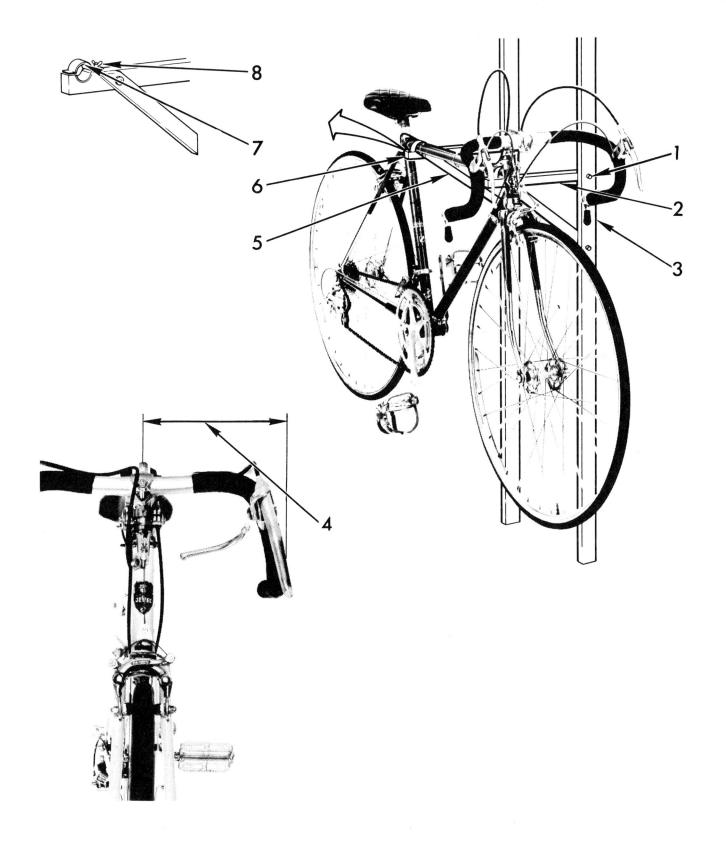

CONSTRUCT MAINTENANCE RACK

Notches (6) or bevels (4) must be cut to fit size of top tube (11) or frame (1).

1. Cut notch (6) or bevel (4) approximately 2 inches from ends of top braces (5,3).

2. Install bicycle clamps (7,2). Line clamp surface with protective material, if desired.

3. Attach support braces (8) to top braces (5,3) so that angle (9) is 45°.

4. Cut ends of support braces (8) to keep 45° angle (9) when rack is installed on rack supports (10).

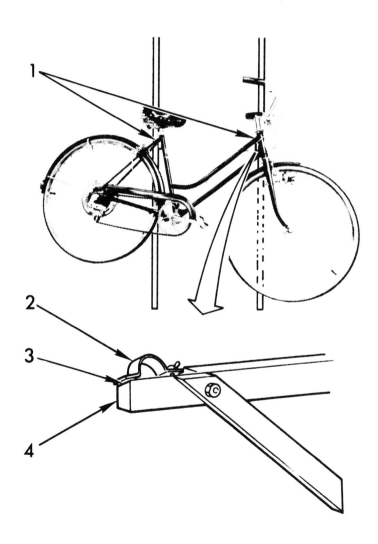

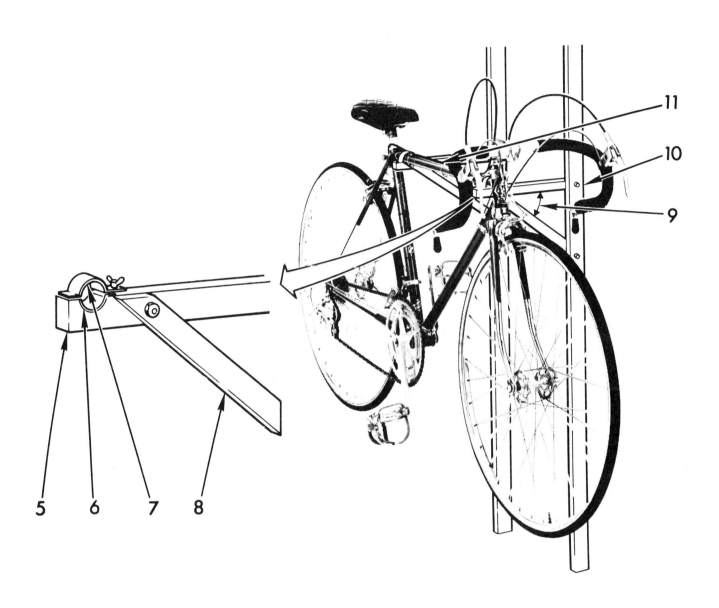

CONSTRUCT MAINTENANCE RACK

Top braces (5) should be installed on rack supports (6) so that distance (3) (see Page 124) is following:

Men's bicycle — Length of top tube (8)

Women's bicycle — Distance between seat tube (1) and headset tube (2)

Top braces (5) should be installed to support bicycle above floor. When working on bicycle, axles (7) should be approximately 2 inches below your elbow.

1.   Measure and locate position for top braces (5). Attach braces to rack supports (6).

2.   Attach support braces (4) to rack supports (6).

CONSTRUCT ENDS HERE

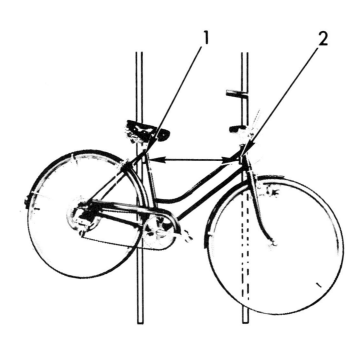

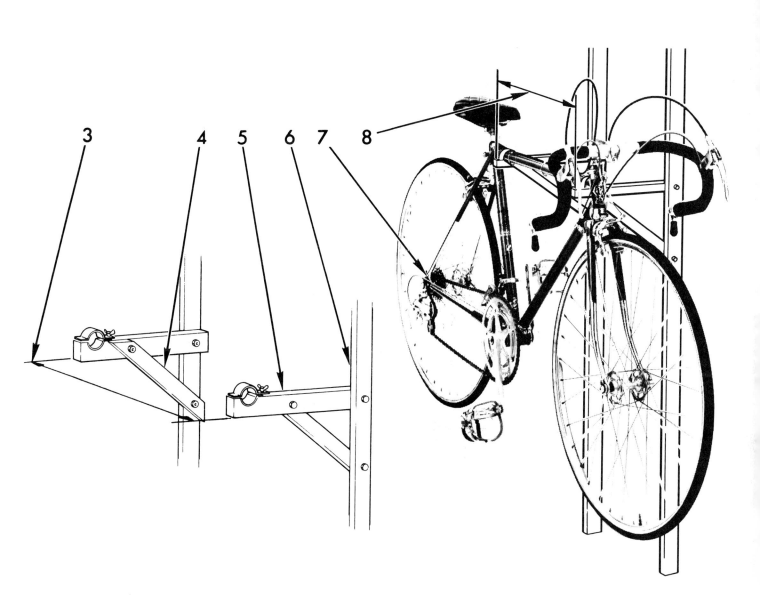

NOTES

NOTES

NOTES

NOTES

NOTES

NOTES

NOTES

Catalog

If you are interested in a list of fine Paperback
books, covering a wide range of subjects
and interests, send your name and address,
requesting your free catalog, to:

McGraw-Hill Paperbacks
1221 Avenue of Americas
New York, N.Y. 10020

How to maintain and repair your 5, 10, & 15-speed bicycle